The Professional Chef's®
Knife Kit

The Professional Chef's®
Knife Kit

THE
CULINARY
INSTITUTE
OF AMERICA®
1946

PREPARATION IS EVERYTHING℠

JOHN WILEY & SONS, INC.
New York • Chichester • Weinheim
Brisbane • Singapore • Toronto

Editorial Team
Jennifer Armentrout
Jessica Bard
Mary Cowell
Mary Donovan
Tim Ryan, CMC
Henry Woods

Photography Team
Dawn Altomari-Rathjen
Elizabeth Corbett Johnson
Lorna Smith

Content Leader
Uwe Hestnar, CEC

Content Team
Robert Briggs
Richard Czack, CMC
Ronald DeSantis, CMC
Dieter Doppelfeld, CMC
Michael Garnero
Victor Gielisse, CMC
Steven Giunta, CEC
Nancy Griffin
Tom Griffiths
Pierre LeBlanc
Xavier Le Roux
Anthony Ligouri
Frederic B. Mayo, PhD
Peter Michael, CMC
Mike Pardus
Tim Rodgers

Acknowledgments
CCI/Superior/ICEL
Chicago Cutlery
Connoisseur
Cuisine de France
Dexter-Russell
EdgeCraft Corporation
F. Dick
Forschner
Geisser-Messer
Global Knives
J.A. Henckels
Kyocera America
Messermeister
Warren Cutlery of
    Rhinebeck, NY
Wüsthof-Trident

Library of Congress Cataloging-in-Publication Data:
Culinary Institute of America.
      The professional chef's knife kit / by The Culinary Institute of
America.
            p.   cm.
      Rev. ed. of: The professional chef's knife / Learning Resources
Center of The Culinary Institute of America, 1978.
      Includes bibliography references and index.
      ISBN 0-471-34997-6 (paper : alk. paper)
      1. Knives.   2. Cutting.   I. The Culinary Institute of America.
Professional Chef's Knife.   II. Title.
      TX657.K54C84   1999
      641.5′89—dc21   99-24635

Printed in the United States of America.

10 9 8 7 6 5

Contents

Meat & Poultry   100

Fish & Shellfish   126

Summary   137

Glossary   139

Index   143

Preface

The tools we put into our knife kits and use in the kitchen today are remarkably similar to those developed thousands of years ago. Technical advances and research in the construction of knives and other basic culinary tools has led to refinements in metal alloys, the ability to refine an edge to a specific task, and adjustments to the shape and construction of a blade to prevent fatigue and stress. During all these years, however, the basics of a good tool's shape and function and the skills necessary to use tools properly have remained constant.

The chef's knife, though not the only tool a chef must master, is generally the knife a novice first learns to use, as well as the one a professional picks up most often. This knife is the most versatile tool in any knife kit because of the many ways in which a skilled hand can work it. In order to develop this accomplished hand, it is important to study, analyze, and practice many cutting techniques used in handling your chef's knife. From this good foundation, it is a simple matter to move on to more specialized knives, including slicers and boning and filleting knives. These can all be mastered easily through practice. As you work with your knives, you will develop a rhythm, learn to coordinate hand motions with cutting tasks, and develop a sense of confidence.

I like to think about building self-confidence in knife use to the manner in which swimmers learn to venture into deep waters. You must have respect for the water, but never fear it. If you fear the water, you cannot relax into it. You will fight against it, and end up in danger. A culinarian must respect knives. Respect grows out of an understanding of the knife's qualities—its proper use, its feel in your hand, its inherent dangers. *The Professional Chef's Knife Kit* addresses all that you must know to develop the confidence and expertise necessary to relax into your work. Relaxation is not the same thing as laziness or lack of attention. It is more a feeling of working with the tool rather than against it.

The novice cook will find information about and skills and procedures for using knives properly and safely in the kitchen. Chefs charged with training their staff will find this a useful, thorough training tool, progressing from basic knife-handling skills, such as steeling and sharpening, to more complex meat fabrication and carving techniques.

A knife that fits your hand and is in prime cutting condition feels like a natural part of your hand. When your skills are as practiced and habitual an activity as is driving a car or dialing a phone, you are well on your way to mastery. Here is to your success!

Richard Czack, C.M.C.
Culinary Ambassador
The Culinary Institute of America
October 1999

Knife Basics

Say the word *chef* and you can almost hear the ringing of knives as they flash back and forth on a steel, the rhythmic knocking of a knife chopping, and the whisper of mincing. You can see the gleam of a blade as it flies through an onion. Knives are so much a part of the chef's work that it is impossible to imagine a chef at work without them. As a result, chefs have a strong and personal attachment to their knives.

Today's cooks and chefs have a wide array of cutting tools available to them. A basic selection of tools, the chef's knife kit, is indispensable. Knives (including chef's knives, utility and paring knives, boning and filleting knives, and specialty knives) are part of this selection, along with the appropriate sharpening tools (steels and stones). Other tools, such as peelers, zesters, brushes, palette knives, oyster and clam knives, and metal and wooden spoons, are also so fundamental to kitchen work that they are considered basics.

Stone cutting tools unearthed by the famed archeologist Richard Leaky at the Koobi Fora site in Kenya are believed to be nearly 3 million years old. They are considered the oldest known man-made tools. Before humans learned to mine and smelt metals, knives had to be produced from found materials, primarily flint and obsidian. Flint, a stone particularly suited to taking an edge, was worked to create a thin cutting edge. Obsidian, a volcanic glass, took a better edge, held it longer, and was more durable than flint, but it was not as widely available. Although obsidian flakes are exceptionally sharp and durable, neither flint nor obsidian are perfect materials.

As time went by and the skills necessary to extract pure metals from the mineral deposits above and below the earth were perfected, new materials more suitable for knife blades and other cutting tools were discovered. By about 6500 B.C.E., the skills of mining and extracting soft metals such as copper, lead, and gold from ore had become more widely practiced. These metals were easy to extract from the ore in which they were found and were also soft enough to work while cold. However, these pure metals were too soft to make durable knives for cooking and hunting.

When pure metals are blended with other metals or minerals, metal alloys are created that have their own distinct properties. By about 3500 B.C.E., copper was being combined (alloyed) with tin to form the harder, more utilitarian bronze in some parts of southeastern Asia. The practice spread to Europe by about 1800 B.C.E.

Iron on its own is quite ductile and prone to rusting. It can be blended with other materials to give it greater stiffness and make the metal hard enough to work so that it will take and keep an edge, as well as to resist corrosion. Iron smelting, the first step in producing steel, began around 2000 B.C.E., although tools made from steel were not widely available at first because early steel-making processes were difficult and dangerous.

TIMELINE OF METALWORKING AND TOOLMAKING

38,000 B.C.E.	Tools made of stone, bone, and horn used.
9000 B.C.E.	New Stone Age begins in Egypt and Mesopotamia.
5500 B.C.E.	Copper smelted from malachite (copper carbonate) in Persia. This metal can be drawn and molded but is too soft to take an edge.
3600 B.C.E.	Bronze made by Southwest Asia artisans. First metal strong enough to hold an edge. Made of copper (80 to 95%) and tin (5 to 20%).
2500 B.C.E.	Iron Age dawns in Middle East when iron is smelted. Temperatures of 1500°C required to smelt. Won't come into wide use for another thousand years. (Egypt and Mesopotamia are well into the Bronze Age; Central Europe and the British Isles are only now entering the Stone Age.)
1400 B.C.E.	Iron Age begins in Asia Minor when an economical method for smelting iron on a larger scale is found.
1000 B.C.E.	Iron Age arrives in Europe in the Hallstatt region of what is today Austria. Iron tools and weapons begin to spread throughout Europe.
475 B.C.E.	Iron comes into use in China.
1709 C.E.	Abraham Darby discovers that coke (made from coal) can be used to fire furnaces used in smelting iron.
1722 C.E.	*L'Art de convertier le fer forgé en acier et l'art d'adoucir*—one of the first treatises on metallurgy in Europe—is written by René Antoin Ferchault de Reamur.
1723 C.E.	Air furnaces are used to smelt iron near Fredericksburg, Virginia, using bituminous coal.
1740 C.E.	Crucible steel rediscovered by Benjamin Huntsman at Sheffield; makes Sheffield steel as famous as Damascus steel (described by Aristotle in 334 B.C.E.).
1754 C.E.	First iron rolling mill established at Foreham in Hampshire, England.
1811 C.E.	Krupp Gustahlfabrik (a factory for the manufacture of English cast steel and all articles made from it) founded in Essen, Germany.
1828 C.E.	Scottish inventor James Beaumont Neilson devises blast furnace.
1831 C.E.	Patent for making malleable cast iron issued to U.S. inventor Seth Boyden.
1837 C.E.	Alfred Krupp visits Sheffield, England, and meets J.A. Henckels, founder of a steel mill in the Ruhr Valley at the town of Solingen.
1839 C.E.	Scottish engineer James Masmyth invents steam hammer; makes larger forging possible without loss of precision.
1851 C.E.	Alfred Krupp exhibits a 4300-ton ingot cast in one piece at London's Great Exhibition.
1856 C.E.	Bessemer converter decarbonizes melted pig iron.
1860 C.E.	Open-hearth process for making steel developed almost simultaneously by German-born British inventor William Siemens and French engineer Pierre Emil Martin.
1868 C.E.	Tungsten steel invented by English metallurgist Robert Forester Mushet.
1882 C.E.	English metallurgist Robert Abbott Hadfield invents manganese steel.
1888 C.E.	Nickel steel invented in France gives impetus to Samuel J. Ritchie's Canadian Copper Company.
1898 C.E.	Frederick Winslow Taylor and Mansuel White, two Philadelphia engineers, develop the Taylor/White process for heat-treating high-speed tool steels, increasing cutting capacities of blade edges by 200–300%.

Adapted from *The People's Chronology* by James Trager, © 1994, Henry Holt and Company Inc.

Early versions of steel show some of the refinements possible when iron is blended with carbon (in the form of ash residue from the forge's fuel left in contact with the iron). As metalsmiths learned to control the amount of carbon added to the iron, a metal known as carbon steel was developed. Low-carbon steel (resembling modern-day wrought iron) was first developed in the Middle East circa 1000 B.C.E., but it was not until 700 B.C.E. that steel tools became common throughout Europe, Asia, and North Africa. Made mostly in small forges and for the purpose of weaponry, the design and production of knives stayed much the same until cutlery for the purpose of dining began to appear in the homes of the nobility. By the sixteenth century C.E., knives, as well as spoons and forks, were established parts of European culture.

Although there was still a great deal more to learn about creating a metal that was durable, flexible, and able to take and hold a sharp edge, these preliminary advances in metal manufacture and the production of tools and knives paved the way for the development of cutting tools similar in nearly all respects to the fine tools used by professional chefs and home cooks today.

Gradual improvements in furnaces allowed metalsmiths to better control the amount of the carbon added to steel. Near the end of the nineteenth century C.E., several rapid advances in steel manufacturing led to the large-scale production of carbon steel of consistent quality. As carbon steel became widely available and affordable, knives made from this material became the norm. This remained the case until the early 1900s, since carbon steel's specific advantages make it well suited to kitchen work. It is durable and hard enough to take an edge but soft enough to allow for reshaping the edge with steels or sharpening stones. If the metal is carefully tempered (subjected to a prescribed series of temperature ranges), it can be made flexible enough for most kitchen work.

Despite all its clear advantages over other materials used to make kitchen knives, there are still some disadvantages to carbon steel. Although it takes a good edge with little effort, the edge deteriorates relatively quickly. This means carbon knives require more upkeep. Carbon steel also rusts, pits, and becomes stained in contact with water and high-acid foods. These knives require careful cleaning and drying before storage, even for a short period.

In 1912, it was discovered that adding chromium to carbon steel inhibits rusting and staining. This metal is called *stainless steel*. However, stainless steel is harder than carbon steel, making it more difficult for kitchen workers to keep the blade's edge in good shape. Although some specialty knives are still made from stainless steel today, as are many surgical instruments, it wasn't until the development of high-carbon stainless steel around 1920 that carbon steel was replaced as the metal of choice for kitchen blades.

Carbon steel chef's knife

High-carbon stainless steel is produced by blending iron, carbon, chromium, and other metals, such as molybdenum, in a specific ratio to form a blade that is stainless, resilient, and capable of receiving and holding a sharp edge. Although other blade materials, such as stainless-steel alloys (the so-called super stainless steel) and ceramic blades, have since been discovered, high-carbon stainless steel is still used to make the majority of professional-quality knives today.

High-carbon stainless steel chef's knife

Ceramic chef's knife

The importance of knives to a professional chef or cook cannot be overstated. High-quality, well-made, well-maintained knives are fundamental kitchen tools that form the foundation of a professional's work. A true professional could get good, even great results from a lesser-quality knife, but it is harder work. Those same tools in the hands of a novice might make work discouragingly difficult, even impossible. The best tools make it easier for the beginner to learn cutting skills properly, right from the start. It is well worth spending the time and money necessary to get a good knife and become comfortable with the skills involved in sharpening, steeling, and using knives for a variety of cutting tasks.

The chef's knife, as the most basic, all-purpose knife, shares similarities with many other knives, from paring knives to boning knives, scimitars to slicers. Even cleavers are made up of the same basic parts. The following discussion of the parts of a knife uses a chef's knife as the model of the typical knife, made up of a blade and a handle. Knowing how each of these parts can be manufactured and shaped will help you to select any knife with care.

The Parts of a Knife

A knife is constructed from several parts, each of which plays a role in the utility, balance, and longevity of the whole. Newer materials have replaced some traditional ones; bone handles are not ordinarily found on kitchen knives today, for example, but composition materials are increasingly common. This section describes the function of each part of the knife and how the parts are put together to form a high-quality tool.

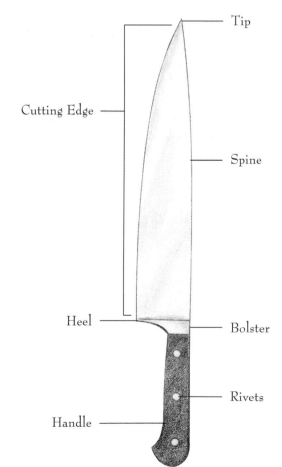

Tip

Cutting Edge

Spine

Heel

Bolster

Rivets

Handle

THE BLADE

Metal knife blades are either forged or stamped.

Forged blades are made by heating a rod (also referred to as a bar or ingot) of high-carbon stainless steel to around 1700°F. The heated metal is dropped into a mold, then struck with a hammer to pound it to the correct shape and thickness. One of the advantages of a forged blade is that its thickness tapers from the spine to the edge and from the heel to the tip, which gives it the correct balance. After the blade is shaped, it is tempered to improve its strength and durability. Forged blades are generally more durable, better balanced, and of good quality. They tend to be more expensive than stamped blades, however.

Stamped blades are made by cutting blade-shaped pieces from sheets of previously milled steel. These blades are of a uniform thickness and may be lighter than some forged blades. Today's stamped blade knives are better balanced than their predecessors, and improved techniques for tempering the metal used has also improved their durability and quality.

After the blade is shaped by either forging or stamping, the edge is created. Several types of edges can be used to create a knife, depending upon the intended use.

Taper ground edge

The sides of the blade taper smoothly from the blade's thickest point, at the spine, to a narrow V-shaped edge. The angle of the V can be gentle or extremely severe, almost wedge-like. Taper ground blades are well-suited to general purpose knives and those used for heavy cutting and chopping work since they keep the blade quite stable.

Making a forged knife (starting from top): metal is shaped in a mold; the metal is cut free from the mold; blade and tang are shaped and tempered; the handle is molded on; the finished knife (Photo courtesy of EdgeCraft Corporation)

Hollow ground edge

The sides of the blade near the edge are ground away to form a hollow, giving the blade an extremely sharp edge. The greater the arc of the hollow, the sharper the edge. Hollow ground blades are well suited to carving and slicing tasks.

Serrated or sawtooth edge

The edge is shaped into a row of teeth that can be set very closely or more widely apart. Teeth that can bite make this a good edge for slicing foods with a crust or a firm skin, such as bread, tomatoes, and melons.

Scalloped edge

The edge is ground into a series of small arcs, making it easier to grip and cut into foods. Scalloped blades are used for slicing many of the same foods as serrated blades.

Granton edge

This edge is made by grinding ovals into the sides of the blade, alternating the position on either side of the blade. This makes it less likely that moist cooked meats and fish, especially smoked salmon or gravlax, will stick to the blade.

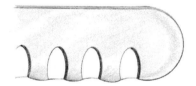

Single-sided edge

Some edges are ground on just one side, especially Japanese-style cutting knives and cleavers.

THE BOLSTER

In some knives there is a collar or shank, known as a *bolster*, at the point where the blade meets the handle. The bolster gives the blade greater stability and strength. This is a sign of a well-made knife, one that will hold up for a long time. Some knives may have a collar that looks like a bolster but is actually a separate piece attached to the handle. These knives tend to come apart easily and should be avoided.

THE TANG

The tang is actually a part of the blade itself. It is the point at which the handle is attached to the knife. Tangs may be full or partial.

A full tang extends the entire length of the handle, giving the knife a greater heft in the handle. Knives with a full tang are sturdy, well balanced, and long lasting. Full tangs are essential for heavy work; chef's knives or cleavers should have a full tang.

A partial tang does not run the full length of the handle. Although blades with partial tangs are not as durable as those with full tangs, they are acceptable for less frequently used knives or those used for lighter work, such as bread knives, paring or utility knives, and some slicers.

Rat-tail tangs are much thinner than the spine of the blade and are encased in the handle, which means that they are not visible at the top or bottom edges. These tangs tend not to hold up under extended use.

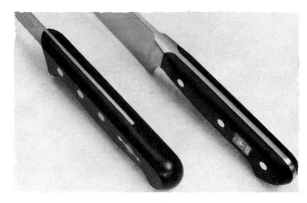

Partial tang (left), full tang (right)

Rat-tail tang

THE HANDLE

Knife handles are made of various materials, including hard woods with very tight grain, such as walnut and rosewood (often impregnated with plastic), textured metal, and composition materials (vinyl). Some are cushioned to make long hours of work less fatiguing.

Wooden handles are attached to the blade with rivets. If rivets are visible on the handle (they are not always), they should lie flush with the surface of the handle to prevent irritation to the hand and to avoid creating pockets where microorganisms could gather. Composition handles are molded onto the tang.

You will hold your knife for extended periods, so be sure the material and the shape of the handle feels comfortable in your hand. Many manufacturers produce several lines of knives so they can offer a range of handle sizes. People with very small or very large hands should be sure that they are not straining their grip to hold the handle.

A variety of knife handles

Types of Knives

As you learn to work in a professional kitchen, you will want to have the correct tools for certain tasks, but that does not mean that you need to acquire every knife under the sun in order to do most kitchen tasks efficiently. You should decide to purchase a special knife only after evaluating whether your work requires it.

The list below is intended as a guide to the knives that may be found in nearly any well-outfitted knife kit. As you continue to learn more about cutting and cooking, you may want or need to acquire some highly specialized knives and cutting tools, such as those used almost exclusively in the bakeshop or butcher shop.

CHEF'S KNIFE

A chef's knife (also known as a *French knife*) is the most often used item in any knife kit. It is designed and manufactured for wide-ranging general use in the kitchen. The blade is shaped and worked so that it can peel and trim, slice, chop, mince, fillet fish, and fabricate meats and poultry. In the hands of a skilled professional, this knife can be used to perform the tasks of many special-purpose knives.

The blade typically ranges from 8 to 12 inches in length and is about $1^1/2$ to 2 inches wide at the heel or bolster, tapering to a point at the tip. When viewed from above, the spine should also appear to taper from its thickest point, at the bolster, toward the tip.

A good-quality chef's knife should be well balanced, with the weight of the blade equaled by the weight of the handle. The handle and the blade should meet in such a way that you can chop foods on a cutting board without bashing your knuckles into the cutting surface. If possible, use a chef's knife to cut something before you buy it to determine which style of knife is best for you.

The blade of the chef's knife has several distinct work areas: the tip, the cutting edge, the heel, the point, the spine, and the flat of the blade.

The tip is used for fine work, paring, trimming, and peeling. It can also be used to core fruits and vegetables or to score items so that they will marinate or cook more evenly.

The cutting edge is used for slicing tasks, such as cutting fish fillets into portions or carving cooked foods into slices. Cutting foods into neat dice, julienne, paysanne, and other precision cuts is easiest when you let the middle portion of the blade's long, sharp, cutting edge do the work.

The heel area of the blade is best suited to cutting tasks that require some force, as the blade is the widest and the thickest at that point. The bolster is located at the heel of the blade, just where the handle and blade meet. The added heft provides the greatest possible concentration of weight and force at that spot in the blade. This permits you to chop through tendons and joints using a quick, sharp motion, or to slice through a winter squash's tough rind.

Even the parts of the blade without an edge have applications in the kitchen. The spine can be used to lightly score foods before pounding or butterflying them, or to crack lobster claws. The flat side of the blade can be used to crush garlic or to lift foods up from the cutting surface.

UTILITY KNIFE

This smaller version of a chef's knife is used for light cutting, slicing, and peeling chores. The blade is generally 5 to 7 inches long. Not only is the blade shorter than that of a chef's knife, it is also thinner and lighter, making it useful for slicing smaller items, such as tomatoes.

PARING KNIFE

Paring knives are the second most often used knife. This knife, used primarily for paring and trimming vegetables and fruits, has a 2- to 4-inch blade. Some blades taper to a point much as a chef's knife; others have a curve or bend at the tip, sometimes referred to as a Granny knife. This knife is a frequently used item, and you should take the time to select a well-made paring knife.

A tournée knife is similar in size to a paring knife, but the blade is curved to make cutting the rounded surfaces of tournéed vegetables easier. The inverted curve of the blade gives this knife its second name, bird's beak.

BONING KNIFE

A boning knife is used to separate raw meat from the bone. The blade is thinner and shorter than the blade of a chef's knife—about 6 inches long—and is usually rigid. Some boning knives have an upward curve; others are straight. The blade is narrower than a chef's knife blade to make it easier to work around bones, between muscle groups, and under gristle and silverskin. Even if this knife is used less frequently than your chef's knife, you should still look for a high-quality boning knife with good stability and durability.

FILLETING KNIFE

Chef's knives and boning knives can be used to fillet fish, but these larger and more rigid blades often leave behind the flesh closest to the bone. Filleting knives are specifically designed for filleting fish. This knife is similar in shape and size to a boning knife, but has a more flexible blade. This permits you to separate the delicate flesh of a fish from the bones easily, with little loss of edible fish.

SLICER

Slicers have long, thin, narrow blades in order to make smooth slices in a single stroke. The type of edge on the blade is selected to make a particular food easier to slice. Some blades are quite flexible and others are rigid, depending upon the food they are used to slice.

Meat slicers are typically 15 to 18 inches long or longer, with taper ground or hollow ground edges and relatively rigid blades. Salmon slicers, used for smoked salmon or gravlax, are even thinner than meat slicers and often have a granton edge to keep the moist, delicate flesh from sticking and tearing as it is sliced. These slicers generally have flexible blades. Slicers used for tomatoes, breads, or pastries are often serrated, scalloped, or saw-toothed.

The tip of the slicer can be pointed or rounded.

CLEAVER

Cleavers have a rectangular blade (the edge may be curved or straight, depending upon intended use) and vary in size and heft.

Japanese- or Chinese-style cleavers are used for the same applications as a chef's knife—to slice, chop, trim, dice, disjoint birds and rabbits, fillet and portion fish, and so forth. These cleavers usually have a single-sided edge.

SCIMITAR

The long curved blade of a scimitar makes it well-suited to the slicing action required to cut through large cuts of raw meat when portioning them into steaks, cutlets, or medallions. The blade can range in length from 12 to 16 inches. This is not generally considered a basic knife, as, unfortunately, fewer and fewer kitchens are butchering and fabricating their own meats today.

Sharpening and Honing Tools

No knife kit can be considered complete without sharpening and honing tools, because the key to the proper and efficient use of any knife is making sure that it stays sharp. (Instructions for steeling and sharpening knives can be found on pages 28–31.) Knife blades are given an edge on a sharpening stone and maintained between sharpenings by honing with a steel.

Sharpening stones
(clockwise from top left):
a) ceramic, b) waterstone,
c) carborundum/aluminum oxide,
d) silicon carbide, e) diamond,
f) Arkansas

SHARPENING STONES

Stones are available in a variety of sizes, textures, and materials. Sharpening stones are produced from such man-made and natural materials as carborundum, silicon carbide, aluminum oxide, ceramic, whetstone, industrial diamond, and naturally occurring sandstone or Arkansas stone—a hard stone quarried from the Ozark Mountains.

The relative coarseness or fineness of the stone's material is referred to as its *grit*. The stone's grit determines degrees of fineness for the edge. Large stones—some with several sides and a reservoir for lubricating oil—have the advantage of accommodating large and heavy blades. Smaller stones may be a bit difficult to use on longer knives but are much easier to transport.

STEELS

Steels are available in coarse, medium, and fine grains. They may be round or oval and are made in varying lengths and diameters. The length of the steel's working surface can range from 3 inches for a pocket version to over 14 inches. The easiest and safest length for a steel is at least 2 to 3 inches longer than the blade of your chef's knife.

Hard steel is the traditional material for steels. Other materials, such as glass, ceramic, and diamond-impregnated surfaces, are also available. Those made of metal are magnetic, which helps the blade retain proper alignment and also collects metal shavings. Ceramic and diamond-impregnated steels are not magnetic.

A guard or hilt between the steel and the handle protects the user, and a ring on the bottom of the handle can be used to hang the steel.

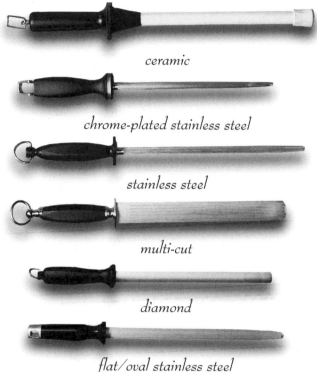

ceramic

chrome-plated stainless steel

stainless steel

multi-cut

diamond

flat/oval stainless steel

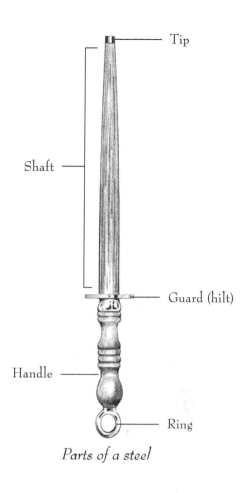

Tip

Shaft

Guard (hilt)

Handle

Ring

Parts of a steel

Electric Knife Sharpeners

Most electric sharpeners use a rapidly rotating abrasive surface that wears away the knife's damaged edge to form a new, sharper edge. The abrasive surface can be a belt, wheel, or series of disks.

Because they operate at high speeds, there is a danger of oversharpening the blade. Even a short time in an electric sharpener can grind away too much of the blade, causing excessive wear and significantly shortening the knife's useful life.

If your kitchen has an electric knife sharpener, be sure to get clear instructions on how to use the sharpener for the best possible results and the least damage to your knife.

Additional Cutting Tools for the Knife Kit

A number of cutting tools are used in the kitchen, some found in a typical knife kit, others in the kitchen itself. Some of these tools make large-volume work easier, faster, and more efficient. Others are used to perform very specific cutting tasks. The tools covered in this section are used to slice, dice, cut, shred, or grate foods.

SMALL TOOLS

A number of small tools other than knives belong either in your knife kit or as part of the kitchen's general tool inventory. It should be noted that, in addition to the hand tools listed here, many others are used in the professional kitchen for various specific functions.

The items shown on the facing page include:

- a set of round cutters, to cut puff pastry and other doughs to the desired shape and to shape or mold foods

- pastry tips and a pastry bag, to pipe creams, purées, and similar items for portioning and presentation

- a zester, to cut away thin strips of vegetable or fruit peels. Zesters are used to obtain the flavorful zest of citrus peels without the bitter pith.

- a plastic scraper, to transfer batters or doughs from bowls and to mix items

- a bench scraper, to transfer cut items to storage containers or cooking vessels, as well as to clean off the board

- an apple corer, to remove cores, leaving the fruit's skin intact. The apple can then be cut into rings or baked whole.

- a channel knife, to score the skin or rind of vegetables and fruits, and for other decorative cuts

- an instant-read thermometer. (The version shown reads 0°F to 220°F; deep-fat and candy thermometers read temperatures up to 600°F.)

- olive and cherry pitters, which remove the pit by plunging a small rod through the olive or cherry, pushing the pit out

a) Pastry bag with tip,
b) bench scraper, c) plastic
scraper, d) olive pitter, e) cherry
pitter, f) rotary peeler, g) measuring spoons, h) instant-read
thermometer, i) pastry brush,
j) small metal offset spatula,
k) channel knife, l) corer,
m) melon baller, n) zester,
o) set of round cutters

- measuring spoons, to accurately measure small amounts of critical ingredients

- a peeler, to remove the peel or skin from vegetables and fruits. Some peelers have fixed blades; other have blades that swivel—these are sometimes referred to as *rotary peelers*. The swivel action accommodates the contours of the item being peeled. Because there are blades on both sides of the peeler, it can be used in both an upward and downward stroke, to make peeling tasks faster.

- a pastry brush, to apply glazes, eggwash, marinades, and toppings

- a small offset spatula, to spread fillings, butters, creams, and similar items.

The items shown on this page include a variety of spatulas. The term *spatula* derives from the same root word that gave us sword, spoon, and spade. The blade may be broad or narrow, flat or bent, metal or rubber. Here are:

- a metal spatula, or palette knife, to spread, turn, or lift items and to transfer items from the cutting surface

- a kitchen fork, to steady foods as they are cut and to test doneness of braised meats. Kitchen forks typically have two prongs that may be curved or flat and narrow, as shown here.

- a rubber spatula (silicon versions and heat-resistant materials are also available), to fold batters, spread items, and transfer items cleanly from working surfaces or containers

- a solid kitchen spoon, a slotted kitchen spoon, and wooden spoons of various sizes, to stir and mix foods

- an offset spatula and tongs, for turning foods as they grill or sauté

- a whisk, for mixing and blending, whipping egg whites and cream, and similar tasks.

a) Large perforated offset metal spatula, b) tongs, c) wire whisk, d) long metal spatula, e) kitchen fork, f) rubber spatula, g) large metal kitchen spoon, h) large metal slotted spoon, i) wooden spoon

The items shown on this page include:

- a fish scaler, to scrape scales from whole fish before filleting

- oyster and clam knives, to pry open shells. The blades are short and extremely rigid. Clam knives are often rounded with a blade that is nearly the same width from one end to the other. Oyster knives tend to have a more pronounced point and a blade that is triangular in shape (or snub-nosed).

- needlenose pliers to remove pinbones from fish

- scissors, to cut grapes into clusters, trim and mince herbs, and cut string. They are also useful to cut through small bones and shells. Poultry shears are also available; they can be quite helpful when cutting through the tight joints and ligaments of chickens, ducks, and geese.

- a shrimp deveiner, to remove the shell and vein from shrimp in a single motion

- a wire mesh glove, to protect your hand when shucking clams and oysters.

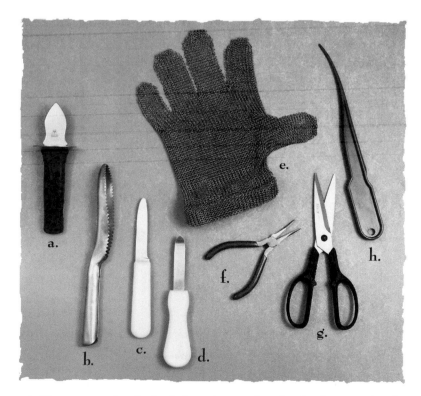

a) Short oyster knife, b) fish scaler, c) clam knife, d) oyster knife, e) metal mesh glove, f) needlenose pliers, g) kitchen scissors, h) shrimp deveiner

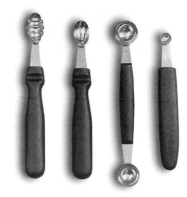

Parisienne scoop (melon baller)

Parisienne scoops are specifically designed for scooping out balls or ovals (depending upon the shape of the scoop) of vegetables and fruits. The scoops are made in a range of sizes and may be round or oval, fluted or smooth.

Grater

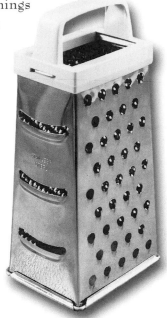

Box graters have four sides with openings of different sizes and shapes on each side. The smaller the hole, the finer the food can be grated. The finest side is used for foods such as hard cheese, citrus zest, and nutmeg. Large openings are used to grate or shred foods of a moderately firm texture.

Nutmeg graters have a curved surface and small openings. Graters for hard cheese, such as the Mouli grater, have a drum pierced with holes that are turned against the food.

For large-volume work, grating attachments are available for mixers, grinders, buffalo choppers, and food processors.

Mandoline

The French-style mandoline is a slicing device made of nickel-plated stainless steel with blades of high-carbon steel. Levers adjust the blades to achieve the cut and thickness desired. As with food slicers, there is a hand guard—the carriage device that holds the food—that is used to prevent injury. The mandoline can be used to make such cuts as slices, juliennes, gaufrettes, and batonnets.

A smaller tool, similar to the mandoline, known as a *Japanese-style mandoline* or *Benriner*, is also widely used in professional and home kitchens (see page 50). The blade is made of stainless steel, but the rest of the cutter is made of plastic, making it less expensive than the traditional mandoline.

Large pieces of equipment with moving blades can be extremely dangerous if they are not used with understanding and respect. The importance of observing all the necessary safety precautions cannot be overemphasized. To keep large equipment functioning properly and to prevent injury or accident, you must keep the equipment properly maintained and cleaned.

As these tools are essential for a number of operations, you should be able to use them with confidence. Observe the following guidelines when working with large equipment:

1. Obtain proper instruction in the machine's safe operation. Do not be afraid to ask for extra help.

2. First turn off and then unplug electrical equipment before assembling or breaking down the equipment.

3. Use all safety features. Be sure that lids are secure, hand guards are used, and the machine is stable.

4. Clean and sanitize the equipment thoroughly after each use.

5. Be sure that all pieces of equipment are properly reassembled and left unplugged after each use.

6. Report any problems or malfunctions promptly and alert coworkers to the problem (an "out of order" sign attached to the machine itself is a good approach).

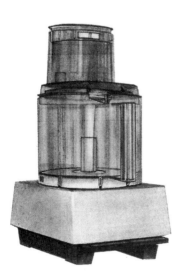

Food processor
A food processor is a processing machine that houses the motor separately from the bowl, blades, and lid. Food processors can grind, purée, blend, emulsify, crush, knead, and, with special disks, slice, julienne, and shred foods.

Electric slicer
This machine is used to slice foods to even thickness. A carrier moves the food back and forth against a circular blade, which is generally carbon steel. There may be separate motors to operate the carrier and the blade. To avoid injury, all the safety features incorporated in a food slicer, especially the hand guard, should be used.

Meat grinder

This is a freestanding machine or an attachment for a standing mixer. A meat grinder should have dies of varying sizes and, in general, has a feed tray and a food pusher (also known as a *tamper*).

The foods should be cut in a size and shape that allows them to drop easily through the feed tube and into the opening only as quickly as the machine can handle them. The tamper should be used only to free foods that stick to the tray or the mouth of the feed tube; it should not be used to force foods down the feed tube.

All food contact areas should be kept scrupulously clean and well chilled. This is important not only for sanitation and wholesome food but also to produce the best possible texture in the finished dish.

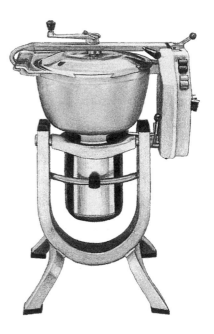

Vertical chopping machine (VCM)

This machine operates on the same principle as a blender. A motor at the base is permanently attached to a bowl with integral blades. As a safety precaution, the hinged lid must be locked in place before the unit will operate. The VCM is used to whip, emulsify, blend, or crush foods.

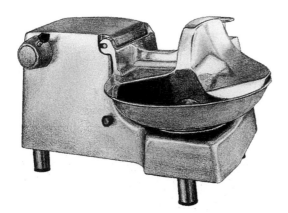

Food chopper (buffalo chopper)

The food is placed in a rotating bowl that passes under a hood, where blades chop the food. Some units have hoppers or feed tubes and interchangeable disks for slicing and grating. Food choppers are available in floor and tabletop models and are generally made of aluminum with a stainless-steel bowl.

Knife Care

Learning to use a knife properly is similar to learning to write your name. At first, you had to concentrate on holding the pencil and shaping each individual letter. As you continued to practice, writing your name became an automatic activity, something occasionally described as "deep knowledge." Today, when you sign a document, you don't think about how you are holding your writing instrument, nor do you consciously shape each letter.

Although penmanship is taught in the same way at the same time to a whole class of students, each individual has a unique signature. So too will you learn to hold your knife and perform cuts in a way that suits your physiology, temperament, and working style.

As with writing, your primary goal is to be as accurate and precise as possible, even if you aren't working at lightning speed.

Eventually, you should acquire both accuracy and speed, but it is not expected that you will have both as you start out. By concentrating on accuracy at first, and not worrying about speed, your deep knowledge of making the various cuts will lead naturally to increased confidence and speed.

Handling and Maintaining Knives

You can always distinguish professional cooks and chefs by the care and attention they lavish on their tools. They keep their knife edges in top shape, honing them frequently as they work, sharpening them on stones, taking them to a knife smith when the edges need to be rebuilt, cradling them in sheaths before stowing them in a kit or drawer. No professional worth his or her salt would dream of dropping a knife into a pot sink or putting a knife away dirty.

Professional pride certainly plays a part in this behavior. More to the point, however, is the professional's sure knowledge that a knife is only valuable as long as it is properly maintained. A well-cared-for knife can make cutting tasks easier to perform. A sharp knife does not require as much effort as a dull one; you really can let the knife cut the food. Clean knives will not contaminate wholesome foods, clean cutting surfaces, or knife kits. They are easier to hold without fear of losing your grip. Knives that are washed by hand don't get chipped or broken under the weight of heavy pots or damaged by the intense heat and chemicals of a dishwasher.

If you have selected your knives carefully, and purchased the best quality knife for the job at hand, you can keep those knives in peak condition by:

- learning and observing the basic rules of knife safety and etiquette

- mastering techniques for honing on a steel and sharpening on a stone

- using the appropriate cutting surface

- cleaning and sanitizing knives as you work

- storing knives properly.

- Always hold a knife by its handle.

- Never attempt to catch a falling knife.

- Never borrow a knife without asking permission, and always return it promptly when you are finished using it.

- When passing a knife to someone else, lay it down on a work surface and allow the other person to pick it up, or pass it handle first (the handle extended to the person receiving the knife).

- Do not allow the blade of a knife to extend over the edge of a table or cutting board.

- Do not use knives to open bottles, loosen drawers, and so on.

- Do not leave knives loose in areas where they cannot easily be seen or wouldn't be found normally (under tables, on shelves, and similar spots).

- If you must carry an unsheathed knife in the kitchen, hold it straight down at your side with the sharp edge facing behind you.

Sharpening Knives on a Stone

Steels are used to realign the edge on your blade. Stones are used to sharpen the edge once it has grown dull through ordinary use.

Opinion is split about whether your knife blade should be run over a stone from heel to tip or tip to heel. Similarly, some chefs prefer to use a lubricant such as mineral oil on their stones, while others swear by water. Like many other aspects of cooking, the "correct" method is a matter of preference and training. Most chefs do agree, however, that consistency in the direction of the stroke used to pass the blade over the stone is important.

Once you find the method that suits you best, be sure to use the same technique every time.

Sharpening: method 1

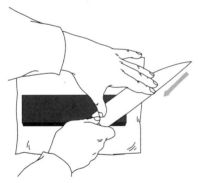

Use four fingers of the guiding hand to maintain constant pressure.

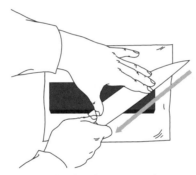

Draw the knife across the stone gently.

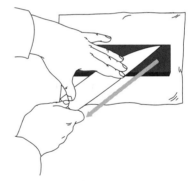

Continue the movement in a smooth action.

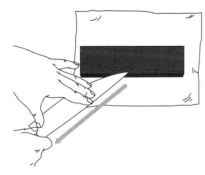

Draw the knife off the stone smoothly.

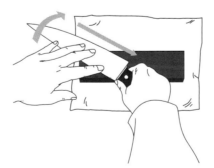

Turn the knife over and repeat the process on the other side.

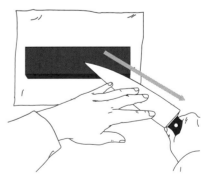

Draw the knife off the stone smoothly.

Before using a stone, be sure that it is properly stabilized. No matter which method you use, keep the following guidelines in mind:

1. Allow yourself enough room to work.

2. Anchor the stone to keep it from slipping as you work. Place carborundum or diamond stones on a dampened cloth or rubber mat. A triple-faced stone is mounted on a rotating framework that can be locked into position so that it cannot move.

3. Lubricate the stone with mineral oil or water. Be consistent about the type of lubricant you use on your stone. Water or mineral oil helps reduce friction as you sharpen your knife. The heat caused by friction may not seem significant, but it can eventually harm the blade.

4. Begin sharpening the edge on the coarsest grit you require. The duller the blade, the coarser the grit should be.

5. Run the entire edge over the surface of the stone, keeping the pressure on the knife even. Hold the knife at the correct angle as you work. A 20-degree angle is suitable for chef's knives and knives with similar blades. You may need to adjust the angle by a few degrees to properly sharpen thinner blades, such as slicers, or thicker blades, such as cleavers.

6. Always sharpen the blade in the same direction. This ensures that the edge remains even and in proper alignment.

7. Make strokes of equal number and equal pressure on each side of the blade. Do not oversharpen the edge on coarse stones. After about ten strokes on each side of the blade, move on to the next finer grit.

8. Finish sharpening on the finest stone and wash the knife thoroughly before use or storage.

Sharpening: method 2

Push the blade over the stone's surface, using the guiding hand to keep pressure even.

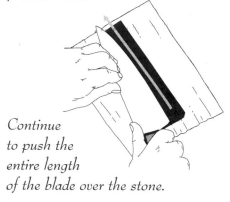

Continue to push the entire length of the blade over the stone.

Push the knife off the stone smoothly.

Turn the knife over and repeat the process on the other side.

Honing Knives on a Steel

Whenever you are using your knives, you should have a steel handy. Get into the habit of using a steel on your knives before you start cutting. Steels are not used to sharpen the edge; they are used to realign it, because with use the edge starts to roll over to one side.

Shown here are two methods for steeling knives. There are yet more techniques you may have an opportunity to learn. Whichever method you choose, these guidelines will help you make effective use of your steel:

1. Allow yourself plenty of room as you work, and stand with your weight evenly distributed. Hold the steel with your thumb and fingers safely behind the guard.

Steeling: method 1

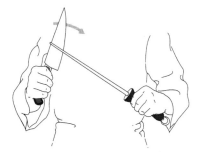

Start with the knife nearly vertical, with the blade resting on the steel's inner side.

Rotate the wrist as the blade moves along the steel.

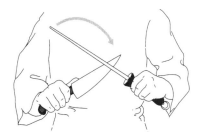

Keep the blade in contact with the steel for the last few inches.

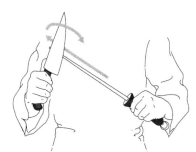

Return the blade to a nearly vertical position, this time on the outer side of the steel.

Use the thumb to maintain even, light pressure.

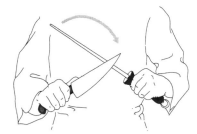

Finish the second pass.

2. Draw the blade along the steel so that the entire edge touches the steel. Work in the same direction on each side of the blade and each time you steel your knife to keep the edge straight.

3. Be sure to keep the pressure even to avoid wearing away the metal in the center of the edge. Over time, this could produce a curve in the edge. Keep the knife blade at a 20-degree angle to the steel.

4. Use a light touch, stroking evenly and consistently. Lay the blade against the steel; don't slap it. Listen for a light ringing sound; a heavy grinding sound indicates that too much pressure is being applied.

5. Repeat the stroke on the opposite side of the edge to properly straighten the edge. If a blade requires more than five strokes per side on a steel, it probably should be sharpened on a stone.

Steeling: method 2

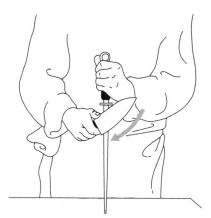

Hold the steel in a near-vertical position with the tip resting on a nonslippery surface. Start with the heel of the knife against one side of the steel.

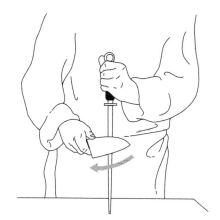

Maintain light pressure and use an arm action, not a wrist action, to draw the knife down the shaft of the steel.

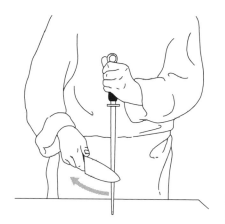

Continue in a smooth motion.

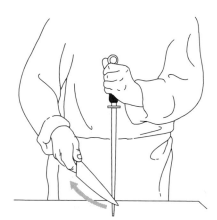

Finish with the knife by drawing it all the way through to the tip.

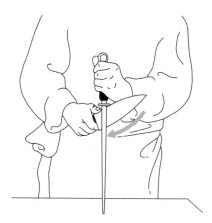

Repeat the action with the blade against the steel's other side.

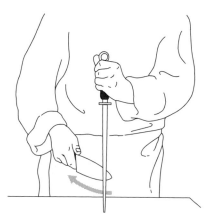

Complete the movement.

Keeping Knives
Clean and Sanitized

Clean knives in hot soapy water and dry thoroughly between cutting tasks as well as after use and before storage. Sanitize them by wiping down the blade and handle with a sanitizing solution as necessary so that the tool does not become a site for food cross-contamination. Keeping knives clean also helps to extend their lives.

Do not clean knives in a dishwasher, because wooden handles are likely to warp and split and edges could be damaged by jostling or temperature extremes.

Never drop a knife into a pot sink. It could be dented or nicked by heavy pots, and someone who reaches into the sink could be seriously injured by the blade.

Cleaning a knife in hot, soapy water

Concentration of Chemical Sanitizers for Double-Strength Sanitizing Solution

Common Name	Chemical Name	Amount per quart of water*
Iodine	Iodophor	2/3 teaspoon per quart water, 25–50 ppm
Chlorine/Bleach	Hypochlorite	3/4 teaspoon per quart of water, 100–200 ppm
Quats	Quaternary Ammonia	200–220 ppm

*This information is meant only as a general guide. Be sure to read and follow dilution instructions provided by the manufacturer.

Cutting Surface

Wooden or composition cutting boards should always be used when cutting foods. Today, many kitchens use color-coded boards to help prevent cross-contamination. Be sure to observe the guidelines of your kitchen. Cutting directly on metal, glass, or marble surfaces will dull and eventually damage the blade of a knife.

Cutting boards should be flat, with a smooth surface. If they become deeply gouged or chipped, they should be either resurfaced or replaced. It is difficult and dangerous to work on a warped cutting board because it cannot be kept stable. To keep the board from slipping or rocking as you work, lay it on a clean dampened side towel or a rubber mat.

Be sure to wipe down the board as you work. This should be done frequently to remove peels, trim, and other debris. When you switch from one type of food to another (from chicken to cabbage, for instance), remember to sanitize the board. Use a clean towel or cleaning cloth that has been wrung out in sanitizing solution. (Concentrations required to make double-strength sanitizing solutions are shown on the facing page.) To prevent your sanitizing solution from becoming dirty too quickly, be sure to wipe down the board with a damp, clean cloth before swabbing with the sanitizing solution.

Stabilizing a cutting board with a damp towel

Wooden versus Composition Cutting Boards

You may have heard a recent controversy about whether composition (plastic or similar materials) boards are cleaner than wooden boards. At first, wood was considered unsanitary, and there was a move toward requiring the use of composition boards.

Further studies indicated that wooden boards were self-healing—that is, small scratches close up enough to prevent bacteria from growing in

them. The bottom line is this: Any board you use should have a smooth surface with no scars, nicks, deep scratches, or gouges.

Wooden boards can be replaned easily to make a new smooth surface. Composition boards are not as easy to resurface and should be discarded if severely damaged. All boards must be thoroughly cleaned, sanitized, and air-dried before storage to keep them safe.

Clean cutting boards carefully after you are finished working on them. Boards should be scrubbed in hot soapy water, rinsed thoroughly, and then submerged in a sanitizing solution for the appropriate amount of time. Once they have drained, cutting boards should be stored in such a way that air can circulate around all surfaces so they will dry thoroughly.

The final stage of washing and sanitizing

Storing cuttings boards so that air may circulate around them

If the cutting surface you use is a large tabletop board, first wipe down the entire board. Bring a container of clean, soapy water to the board and use a scrub brush or scrubbing pad to clean the entire surface carefully. Scrape away the soapy water and any residue that is lifted using a bench scraper. Wipe down the board carefully with a clean, damp cloth to remove any traces of soap. Finally, wipe down the entire surface with a clean cloth that has been wrung out in a sanitizing solution.

Storing Knives

There are a number of safe, practical ways to store knives: in knife kits or cases for one's personal collection, and wall- or tabletop-mounted racks. Proper storage prevents damage to the blade and harm to unwary individuals.

When knives are stored loosely, as in many knife kits and often in drawers, plastic knife guards or handmade sheaths can add an extra level of protection (see "Making Paper Sheaths" on the facing page).

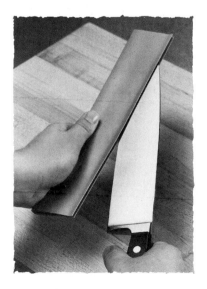

Removing a knife from a plastic sheath

Making Paper Sheaths

Rigid or soft sheaths can be purchased to fit a variety of knives. It is also possible to make sturdy sheaths inexpensively from kraft paper, as shown here.

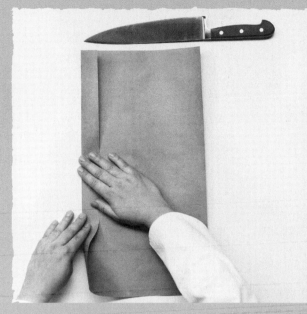

1. Cut a piece of paper that is 1 inch longer than your blade and 18 inches wide. Fold back 1 inch along the entire width of the paper.

2. Lay your knife on the paper, one blade-width in from the edge, along the short side, with the tip inserted into the 1-inch crease. Fold over the short edge to begin wrapping the blade in paper.

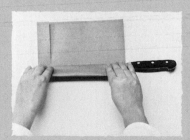

3. Continue to fold the paper, wrapping it around the blade in several layers.

4. Use tape to secure the bottom and top of the sheath; use as many additional pieces of tape as needed to keep the sheath closed.

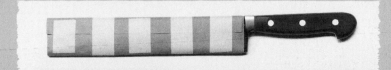

Photos by Mike DiJerian

Designed for the professional chef, a portable case is a safe, convenient home for a large collection of knives and other kitchen utensils. Each knife fits into a particular slot so there is little risk of clanking about. The case shown here is made of vinyl so that it can be easily cleaned and sanitized. Cloth and leather cases (or rolls) cannot be cleaned as easily.

Steel and rubber slotted holders are more sanitary and easier to keep clean than wood slotted holders or blocks. The steel is not porous like wood and cannot harbor microorganisms; the rubber is removable and may be washed and sanitized—even in the dishwasher.

Slotted hangers should always be mounted on the wall, not on the side of a table, as the exposed blade can present a safety hazard.

Steel and rubber slotted knife holder

Other options for storing knives in the kitchen include custom-built drawer systems, slotted to hold the blade securely in place, and magnetized bars, which can be mounted on a wall.

It is sometimes necessary for professional cooks and chefs to travel by air. The fear of losing your knives or having them damaged due to mishandling might make you reluctant to check your knives as regular baggage, but airline safety regulations do not allow them as standard carry-on luggage. Be sure to pack them carefully, with sheaths covering the blades, in a case that keeps them from shifting around during handling. If you are worried that your knives may not make it to your destination with you, call ahead to arrange for a backup kit to be on hand.

The rubber insert pulls out to be washed

Your choice of knife grip depends on the particular task and the specific knife. The four basic grips are shown here:

► Grip the handle with four fingers and hold the thumb firmly against the blade's spine.

► Grip the handle with all four fingers and hold the thumb gently but firmly against the side of the blade.

◄ Grip the handle with three fingers, rest the index finger flat against the blade on one side, and hold the thumb on the opposite side to give additional stability and control.

► Grip the handle overhand, with the knife held vertically. This grip is used with a boning knife for meat fabrication tasks.

Your grip on the knife is determined as much by your personal preference and comfort as it is by the cutting task at hand. The same is true for your guiding hand, the hand responsible for controlling the food you are cutting.

◀ Here is one classic position for the guiding hand. The fingertips are tucked under slightly and hold the object, with the thumb held back from the fingertips. The knife blade then rests against the knuckles, preventing the fingers from being cut.

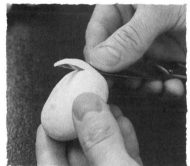

▶ When you peel or trim foods, cut them into tournées, or flute them, you may find yourself holding the food in the air, above the cutting surface. In that case, the guiding hand holds and turns the food against the blade to make the work more efficient. Be sure that the food, your hands, and your knife handle are all very dry.

◀ Certain cutting techniques, such as butterflying meats or slicing a bagel in half, call for the guiding hand to be placed on top of the food to keep it from slipping, while the cut is made into the food parallel or at an angle to the work surface. Holding your hand flat on the upper surface of the food with a little pressure makes these cuts safe to perform.

◀ The guiding hand is also used to hold a carving or kitchen fork when disjointing or carving cooked meats and poultry in front of customers. The tines of the fork can be laid flat on the surface of the food or inserted directly into the item to hold it in place as it is carved.

Basic Cuts

The basic cuts include chopping and mincing, julienne and batonnet, dice, rondelle, and oblique and roll cuts. The aim should always be to cut the food into pieces of uniform shape and size. Evenly cut items look more attractive, but more important, they cook evenly so your dishes have the best possible flavor, color, and texture. The flavor, texture, and appearance of the dish suffers if its components are unevenly cut.

These cuts are illustrated step by step in the following pages. It is important to be completely familiar with these cuts and able to execute them properly. Note that the dimensions indicated throughout this chapter are only guidelines. You may prefer to make your cuts a little thicker or thinner, longer or shorter, depending upon the quality of the product or the specific needs you have when preparing a recipe or establishing plating guidelines.

Set up your work area safely and completely before you start to work.

Your work surface should be a height that doesn't force you to either stoop or reach up at an uncomfortable angle. It should be stable and secure.

Select a cutting board of the appropriate size and check to be sure it is not seriously gouged or chipped. Be sure to adhere to your own kitchen's standard practices, especially if a color-coded cutting board system is in place. For more information about using cutting boards properly, see pages 33–34.

Gather items necessary to keep your work area safe and clean.

Cross-contamination of foods occurs when a contaminated item—for example, a shell egg with salmonella—comes in contact with another surface—another food item, your knife, your cutting board, your towel, your hands, or your gloves. You must destroy or remove the pathogen by cooking the food, washing your hands properly, cleaning and sanitizing tools and work surfaces, and replacing soiled side towels, aprons, and gloves.

Your work station mise en place must include a container of double-strength sanitizing solution, clean wiping clothes, side towels, and gloves.

Gather the appropriate portioning and storage materials.

Have on hand enough containers to hold separately each of the following: prepped items ready to use in other preparations or to serve as is, wholesome trim to use in preparations such as stocks or soups, inedible trim and other refuse. Be sure to have a separate container for composting if your kitchen is equipped to compost food scraps.

Use scales properly.

If part of your prep work includes portioning raw materials, have a scale or other portioning equipment ready, making sure that it is properly cleaned before you begin work. Cover the food contact surface of the scale with plastic wrap, parchment paper, butcher's paper, or deli paper. This makes later cleanup easier, of course, and is also important to help prevent cross-contamination. Be certain to change the wrap between each type of product as well.

Keep foods at the best possible temperature for prep work.

Many foods should be kept well chilled to avoid foodborne illness. Some foods, however, are relatively stable at room temperature. These include most root vegetables; not only are they safe at room temperature, they are easier to cut. However, if you have any doubt about the potential danger of holding any food at room temperature, it is better to err on the side of safety and keep things cold.

Stand in a natural position, facing the cutting board squarely.

You may need to change your stance from time to time, but avoid twisting the trunk of your body in the opposite direction from your legs.

Good posture and general fitness help avoid back strain and general fatigue as you work. Regular exercise can improve posture and fitness as well as strength, flexibility, stamina, and even your ability to concentrate.

Sturdy, supportive shoes are a must, as are good-quality socks that cushion and protect your feet.

Arrange your work so that it flows in a logical direction.

The direction of the flow depends upon whether you are left- or right-handed. The basic rule is to keep all product moving in one direction. You may need to break complex preparation tasks into individual steps.

Use gloves properly.

Since 1992, New York State law requires all food handlers to wear gloves whenever they touch foods that will not be cooked to a safe service temperature before they are served to the customer. Gloves must be used properly if they are to keep the food safe from cross-contamination.

Remember that your gloves are not a magic barrier to pathogens, and they do not take the place of thorough and proper handwashing. Gloves themselves can become contaminated. Do not switch from one food type to another (for example, from sliced turkey to fruit salad) without changing your gloves. If a glove tears or rips, replace it right away. Replace your gloves whenever you have left your station, for any reason.

Your gloves should fit close to your hand. Gloves that are too large may slip as you work. Gloves that are too small will not only be uncomfortable, they will tear easily.

Most foods require some preliminary trimming, peeling, or squaring off to make subsequent cuts easier to perform.

◀ Trimming tasks include and removing root and stem ends from fruits, herbs, and vegetables.

Peeling tasks can be done using a rotary peeler if the skin is not too thick; carrot, potato, and similar skins are easy to remove with a peeler. Remember that these peelers work in both directions. ▶

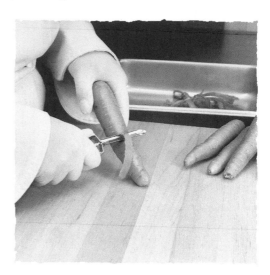

◀ Very young, pencil-thin asparagus does not have to be peeled, but otherwise, you should peel asparagus to remove the tough fibers in the skin and improve its appearance.

Trim the asparagus to remove the woody or fibrous stem ends. To prevent the asparagus from snapping as you peel it, lay it with the stem end near the edge of your work surface. Peel in one direction only, working from the top to the bottom. This will make it easier to peel away the barbs along the stem without snapping off the tip.

▶ Paring knives are used to trim many vegetables and fruits.

A chef's knife is required for vegetables, fruits, and other foods with thick rinds or skins, such as hard-skinned squashes and pineapples. ▶

Exterior fat, gristle, and sinew can be removed from meats and poultry with a boning knife.
▼

Foods that are naturally round can be difficult to control as you cut them. A slice can be removed from the bottom or side of a round food to make it sit flat on the cutting board, as was done to make slicing this potato easier. ▶

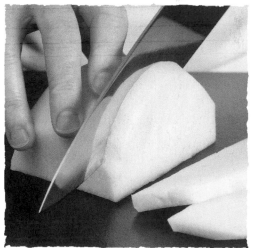

Squaring off is done by cutting away slices from the top and bottom and both sides and ends of round vegetables, such as potatoes and turnips, to give them more regular dimensions, important whenever you are doing precision cutting tasks, such as cutting julienne or dicing (see pages 52–57). Slices can be cut from the ends and top of the vegetable to create a rectangle or square.

To chop a food, you must cut it into pieces that are roughly the same size, but it is not critical to cut them to the exact dimensions called for when you dice or julienne an item. Mirepoix is generally chopped, as are mushrooms and other aromatic vegetables, fruits, or herbs that you will eventually strain out of the item you are preparing, as well as foods that you will purée.

Although the term chopping is sometimes used interchangeably with mincing, there is a distinction. Minced foods are generally cut into a finer size. This is either because the food itself is relatively fine, such as the fresh herbs demonstrated on the facing page, or because the end product is cut into very fine pieces, such as minced shallots, shown on page 66.

1. Trim the root and stem ends and peel the item if necessary.

2. Slice or chop the food at nearly regular intervals until the cuts are relatively uniform. This need not be a perfectly neat cut, but all the pieces should be roughly the same size.

Chopping carrots, onions, and celery into same-size pieces for mirepoix. They are left fairly large here to be used in a long-simmering stock. Cut them smaller for dishes that cook less than an hour.

1. Rinse and dry the herbs well, and strip the leaves from the stem. Gather the herbs in a pile on a cutting board. Use your guiding hand to hold them in place. Position the knife so that it can slice through the pile.

2. Once the herbs are coarsely cut, use the fingertips of your guiding hand to hold the tip of the chef's knife in contact with the cutting board. Keeping the tip of the blade against the cutting board, lower the knife firmly and rapidly, repeatedly cutting through the herbs or vegetables. Continue cutting until desired fineness is attained.

▲ Scallions and chives are minced in a slightly different fashion. Rather than cutting repeatedly through scallions or chives, they are sliced very fine.

Shredded or grated items can be coarse or fine, depending upon the intended use. Foods can be shredded with a chef's knife, a slicer, shredding tools and attachments, a mandoline, or a box grater.

◄ When cutting tight heads of greens, such as Belgian endive and head cabbage, cut the head into halves, quarters, or smaller wedges and remove the core before cutting shreds with a chef's knife. The tip of the knife either remains in contact with the board as you cut or comes in contact with the board as you make a smooth downward slicing stroke. The blade's edge rocks onto and off of the cutting surface with each stroke.

◄ Other tools can be used to shred or grate foods, including the grater attachments found on food processors, mixers, choppers, and box graters. Specialized graters are available for specific tasks, such as nutmeg, cheese, or ginger graters. Be sure to hold the food properly to avoid grating your fingertips and knuckles.

Slicing Cuts: Plain and Decorative

When a knife is properly sharpened, it slices cleanly through food, making your work easier, even effortless. Simply guide the knife through the food, keeping the cut straight and even and letting the knife do the work.

The length of your stroke and the pressure you exert on the food should be adjusted to suit the texture of the food you are slicing. To make a long, smooth stroke, use a knife with a long blade. A salmon slicer is long and thin enough to permit thin slices without sawing the blade back and forth.

To cut through a pâté en croûte, you may need to use a serrated knife for the crust. Because the pastry is delicate and

could shatter, you need to make short back-and-forth cuts until you cut through the crust. Once the top crust has been cut, you may wish to use the index and middle fingers of your guiding hand to hold the slice as you continue to cut. Your strokes should increase in length, and you can exert a little more force on the downward stroke to cut through the pâté.

Galantines and other garnished or filled items need to be sliced carefully to keep the arrangement of the dish intact. You may wish to dip your knife into a container of warm water, which makes it easier to cut cleanly with the least amount of pressure. ▶

If you can make clean, even slices, you can cut boneless cuts of meat into steak or medallions, boneless fish fillets into portions, and carve roasted meats, as shown on pages 119–125. The following pages illustrate how to cut fruits, vegetables, and herbs in a variety of ways.

Chiffonade

The chiffonade cut is done by hand to cut herbs, leafy greens, and other ingredients into very fine shreds. Chiffonade is distinct from shredding, however, in that the cuts are much finer and uniform. This cut is typically used for delicate leafy vegetables and herbs.

1. For greens with large, loose leaves, roll individual leaves into tight cylinders before cutting. Stack several smaller leaves before cutting.

2. Use a chef's knife to make very fine, parallel cuts to produce fine shreds.

Rondelles

Rondelles, or rounds, are simple to cut. The shape is the result of cutting a cylindrical vegetable, such as a carrot, crosswise.

1. Trim and peel the vegetable as necessary.

2. Make parallel slicing cuts through the vegetable at even intervals using a chef's knife, slicer, utility knife, electric slicer, or mandoline.

The rondelle shape can be varied with special tools as shown below:

Ovals, Half-moons, and Flowers

The basic rondelle shape, a round disk, can be varied by cutting the vegetable on the bias to produce an elongated or oval disk, or by slicing the vegetable in half for half-moons. If the vegetable is scored with a channel knife before slicing, a flower is produced. ▼

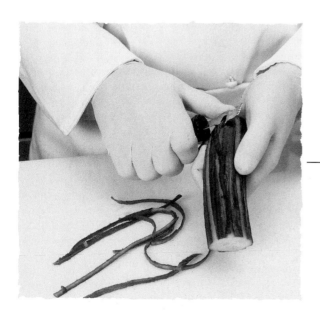 

◀ Ripple Cuts

Special cutters or blades are required to produce ripple cuts. Hand tools and slicers are available for this purpose. The ripple cut blade on a mandoline is used to cut cucumbers here. Special blades are also available for use with food processors, slicers, and choppers.

Gaufrettes ▶

Gaufrette means *waffle*, a good description of this special cut. You need a mandoline to make a gaufrette cut.

1. Set your blades properly so that the slicing blade and the julienne teeth are both opened to the appropriate thickness.

2. Make the first pass, running the vegetable the entire length of the mandoline. Turn the vegetable 90 degrees and repeat the entire stroke. Turn the vegetable 90 degrees each time you complete a pass. These gaufrette sweet potatoes have been deep-fried.

◀ Ribbons

Long, round vegetables, such as soft-skinned squashes and zucchini, can be cut into long, thin slices known as *ribbons* or *noodles*. To prepare the vegetable for slicing, cut it into halves or quarters (depending on its diameter). Adjust your slicer (a Japanese-style mandoline is shown here) to make cuts of the desired thickness, and pass the entire length of the vegetable over the blade to make ribbons. To make noodles, use the serrated blade.

Diagonal ▶

The diagonal cut is often used to prepare vegetables for stir-fries and other Asian-style dishes. Because it exposes a greater surface area of the vegetable, employing this cut shortens cooking time.

1. Place the peeled or trimmed vegetable on the work surface.

2. Make a series of even parallel cuts of the desired thickness, holding the knife so that the cuts are made at an angle to produce the bias.

Oblique or Roll Cut

Oblique, as it refers to a vegetable cut, reflects the fact that the cut sides are neither parallel (side by side) nor perpendicular (at right angles). This effect is achieved by rolling the vegetable after each cut. This cut is used for long, cylindrical vegetables such as parsnips, carrots, and celery. There are no specific dimensions for the oblique cut; the angle at which the cuts are made should be closed or opened, as required, to produce pieces of approximately the same size.

1. Place the peeled vegetable on a cutting board. Make a diagonal cut to remove the stem end.

2. Hold the knife in the same position and roll the vegetable 180 degrees (a half-turn). Slice through it on the same diagonal, forming a piece with two angled edges.

3. Repeat until the entire vegetable has been cut.

Precision and Portioning Cuts

Precision cuts are used when nearly perfect uniformity is required. The ability to produce neat, even cuts shows your skill and craftsmanship, of course. More importantly, it means that foods cook evenly and retain the best possible flavor, nutrition, color, and appearance as they cook.

Portioning cuts are important when creating steaks, scallops, chops, fillets, and other portions of meat, fish, and poultry. Keeping the cuts of a consistent size and shape is important both to keep your customer happy and to keep your food costs low. These cuts are described on pages 54–60.

Fine Julienne
$1/16$ x $1/16$ x 1 to 2 inches

Julienne/Allumette*
$1/8$ x $1/8$ x 1 to 2 inches

Brunoise
$1/8$ x $1/8$ x $1/8$ inch

Small Dice
$1/4$ x $1/4$ x $1/4$ inch

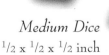

Medium Dice
$1/2$ x $1/2$ x $1/2$ inch

Batonnet
$1/4$ x $1/4$ x 2 to 2 $1/2$ inches

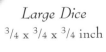

Large Dice
$3/4$ x $3/4$ x $3/4$ inch

*Allumette normally refers only to potatoes

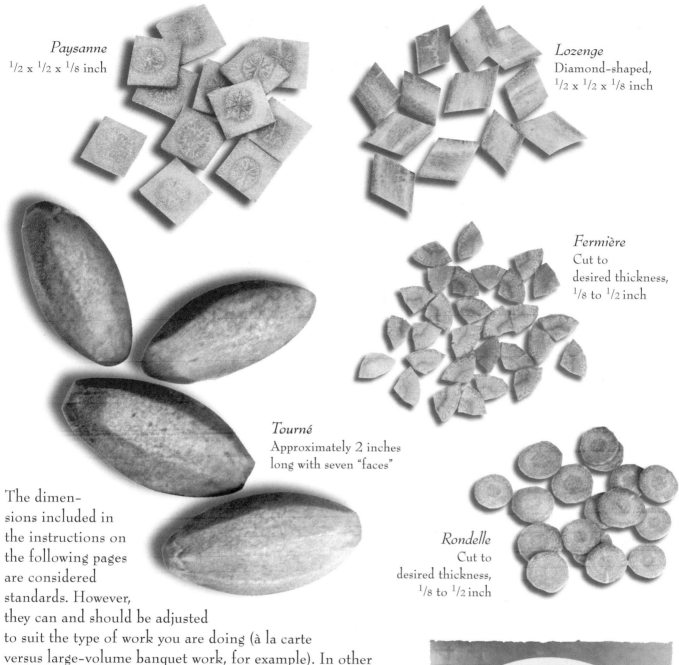

Paysanne
$1/2$ x $1/2$ x $1/8$ inch

Lozenge
Diamond-shaped,
$1/2$ x $1/2$ x $1/8$ inch

Fermière
Cut to
desired thickness,
$1/8$ to $1/2$ inch

Tourné
Approximately 2 inches
long with seven "faces"

Rondelle
Cut to
desired thickness,
$1/8$ to $1/2$ inch

The dimensions included in the instructions on the following pages are considered standards. However, they can and should be adjusted to suit the type of work you are doing (à la carte versus large-volume banquet work, for example). In other words, you may hand-cut foods for small-volume work to exact specifications, while for a banquet, it is more reasonable to use equipment such as slicers, choppers, and other machines to produce reasonably similar sizes.

Another factor to keep in mind when making precision cuts is the way you will serve the food. Even though the standard julienne cut is understood to be $1/8$ inch square and 1 to 2 inches long, you should cut it smaller when the vegetables are served as a soup garnish so they will fit neatly into the bowl of a soupspoon, as shown here.

Julienne and Batonnet

Julienne and batonnet are long, rectangular cuts. Related cuts are the standard pommes frites and pommes pont neuf cuts (both are names for french fries) and the allumette (or matchstick) cut. The differences between these cuts is the size of the final product.

- Julienne cuts are $^1/_8$ inch by $^1/_8$ inch in thickness and 1 to 2 inches long.

- Batonnet is $^1/_4$ inch by $^1/_4$ inch in thickness and 2 to $2^1/_2$ inches long.

These dimensions may be modified slightly to suit a specific need. The key point to keep in mind is that each cut should be nearly identical in dimension to all others for even cooking and the best appearance.

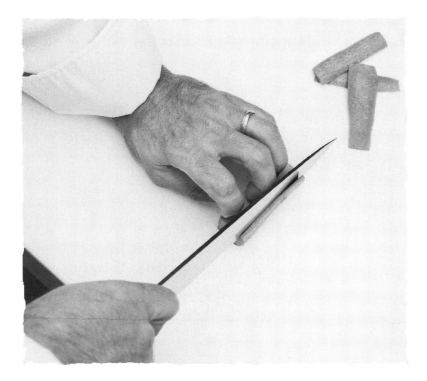

1. Trim the vegetable so that the sides are straight, which makes it easier to produce even cuts. The trimmings can be used, as appropriate, for stocks, soups, purées, or any preparation where shape is not important.

2. Slice the vegetable lengthwise, using parallel cuts of the proper thickness.

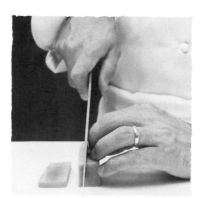

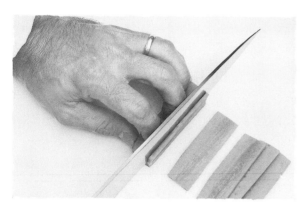

Julienne should be cut to ¹/₈ inch thick

Batonnet should be cut to ¹/₄ inch thick

3. Stack the slices, aligning the edges, and make parallel cuts of the same thickness through the stack. Cuts should be:

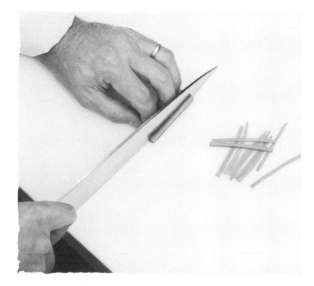

¹/₈ inch apart for julienne

¹/₄ inch apart for batonnet

A few special cuts associated with potatoes are produced
using the same techniques as for julienne:

Pommes pailles (straw potatoes) are an
extremely fine julienne (less than $1/16$
inch square) cut to the desired length.
Straw potatoes can also be cut using a
mandoline to create thin slices. Set
the mandoline to a very narrow opening. Cut the slices into pailles by hand
as shown. ▶

Pommes allumettes (matchstick potatoes), cut to the same dimensions as a
fine julienne, are shown here being cut
on a mandoline, then cooked. ▶

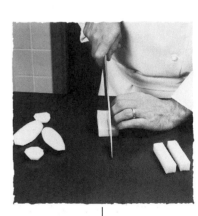

Pommes pont neuf got their name from
their resemblance to a famous bridge in
Paris known as the Pont Neuf, or the
"new bridge." A common English equiv-
alent name is steak fries.

This cut may be performed so that the
rounded edge of the potato is not
trimmed away, thus producing the
bridge shape. ◀

When executed as a precision cut, the
potato is trimmed to create straight
sides. ▶

Dice

Dicing is a cutting technique that produces a cube-shaped product. To prepare foods, first trim and peel as needed. Cut the vegetable into slices of the appropriate thickness, as shown on page 55. The smallest dice is known as *brunoise*. The name derives from the French verb, *brunoir* (to brown), and reflects the common practice of sautéing these finely-diced vegetables. To make larger dice, cut the slices to the thickness that you wish the finished dice to be. Dimensions for the various size dice are noted below the accompanying photographs. The term *cube* refers to cuts ³/₄ inch or greater.

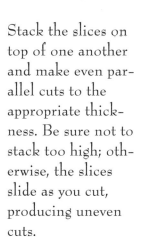

Stack the slices on top of one another and make even parallel cuts to the appropriate thickness. Be sure not to stack too high; otherwise, the slices slide as you cut, producing uneven cuts.

Gather the sticks together; use your guiding hand to hold them in place and make crosswise parallel cuts through the sticks. These cuts should be the same thickness as the initial slices to produce perfectly even, neat dice.

Brunoise (a fine dice) should be ¹/₈ inch square and is derived from julienne cuts

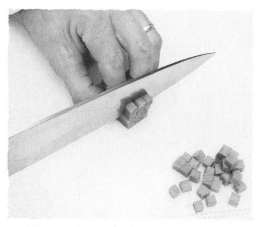

Small dice should be ¹/₄ inch square and is derived from batonnet cuts

Medium dice should be ¹/₃ inch square and is derived from a large batonnet

Large dice should be ³/₄ inch square

Paysanne and Fermière

Cuts produced in the *paysanne* (peasant) or *fermière* (farmer) style are generally used in dishes intended to have a rustic or home-style appeal. When used for traditional regional specialties, you may opt to cut them in such a way that the shape of the vegetable's curved or uneven edges are still apparent in the finished cut. However, it is important that they are cut to the same thickness so that they will cook properly and evenly.

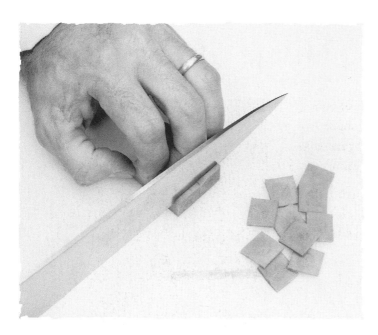

For a more rustic presentation, cut the vegetable into halves, quarters, or eighths, depending on its size. The pieces should be roughly similiar in dimension to a batonnet. Make even, thin crosswise cuts at roughly $1/8$-inch intervals.

In order to feature paysanne or fermière cuts as an ingredient in a classical dish or for a more upscale setting, cut the vegetables in a more precise style as shown here.

Square off the vegetable first and make batonnet that are $1/2$ inch thick. Cut the batonnet crosswise at $1/8$-inch intervals.

Lozenge

The lozenge, or diamond, cut is most often used to prepare a vegetable garnish. To make this cut, make thin slices (generally about $1/4$ inch thick). Cut the slices into strips about $1/2$ inch wide. Holding your knife at an angle to the strip, make parallel cuts that produce a diamond shape.

Decorative Cuts

These cuts are primarily used for garnishes, to improve the appearance of a finished dish, and to give your plates or platters a special look. They typically generate a significant amount of trim. The trim from these items can be put to good use, if you are careful to properly rinse and clean the vegetable. You may peel some items before cutting them into tourné or preparing parisienne-style cuts; the trim then can be used to create purées and coulis. (For more information on these preparations, refer to *The New Professional Chef.*)

Tourné

Turning vegetables (*tourner* in French) requires a series of cuts that simultaneously trim and shape the vegetable. The shape may be similar to a barrel or a football. This is often regarded as one of the most demanding, time-consuming, and exacting cuts.

1. Peel the vegetable, if desired or necessary. If the trimmings can be used with the peel still intact, or if there is no appropriate use for the trimmings, you do not need to peel the vegetable.

2. Cut the vegetable into pieces of manageable size. Cut large round or oval vegetables, such as beets and potatoes, into quarters, sixths, or eighths (depending on their size), into pieces slightly longer than 2 inches. Cut cylindrical vegetables, such as carrots, into 2-inch pieces. To make tournés with flat bottoms and three to four faces, such as with zucchini, cut the vegetable in half before cutting it into sections.

3. Hold the vegetable in your guiding hand. Using a paring knife or tourné knife, carve the pieces into barrel or football shapes.

To produce classic tournés, you should cut the vegetable so that it has seven sides or faces. The faces should be smooth, evenly spaced, and tapered so that both ends are narrower than the center. A form of tournéing that removes the seeds or core from a vegetable can be used with zucchini, cucumbers, and carrots. These tournés generally have four or fewer sides. A selection of tournéed vegetables shows the range of effects that can be produced by adjusting the classic tourné technique to suit various vegetable types. Make certain that, whichever tourné style you use, all the pieces are cut uniformly.

Tourné—continued ▶

POTATO TOURNÉS

Potatoes cut into tournés include pommes château and pommes fondantes (slightly larger than château).

Pommes château (left),
pommes fondantes (right)

Parisiennes

A parisienne scoop (or melon baller) is used to make uniform balls of fruits or vegetables. This can create a significant amount of trim loss. The technique shown here produces the neatest scoops with the least possible loss.

1. Trim or peel the vegetable or fruit so that the solid flesh is exposed.

2. Twist the scoop into the flesh, pushing down to recess it. This produces a round ball, without a flat top. Work to an even depth over the surface of the vegetable or fruit. Once you have removed all the scoops that you can, slice away the scooped part to create a fresh layer that can be scooped again.

Carrots, celeriac, and similar vegetables are peeled first. A straight slice is removed from larger vegetables to expose the interior.

A melon is halved and the seeds are removed before making melon balls.

Fluting

This technique takes some practice to master, but the result makes an attractive garnish. It is customarily used on firm white mushrooms. Some chefs like to pull off the tender skin covering the cap for a very white mushroom.

1. Leave the mushroom stem intact as you flute the cap. This makes it easier to control the mushroom and prevents the cap from falling apart or breaking as you cut. To keep the mushroom clean as you work, cut away the portion of the stem that was growing underground.

2. Hold the mushroom between the guiding hand's thumb and forefinger. Place the blade of a paring knife or a tourné knife at an angle against the mushroom cap center. Rest the thumb of the cutting hand on the mushroom and use it to brace the knife.

3. Rotate the knife toward the cap edge to cut a shallow groove. At the same time the knife blade is cutting, use your guiding hand to turn the mushroom in the opposite direction. (Some chefs like to hold the knife with the blade pointing toward them and make cuts that start at the top of the cap and end at the edge. Others prefer to hold the knife with the blade pointing away from them and make the cuts in the opposite direction, starting at the edge of the cap and finishing at the top.)

4. Turn the mushroom slightly and repeat the cutting steps. Continue until the entire cap is fluted. Pull the trimmings away.

5. Trim away the stem after the cap is fluted.

Vegetables & Fruits

Foods with a uniform texture throughout (once the peel and trim have been removed), such as potatoes, carrots, celery, and turnips, can be cut using the methods illustrated in the preceding sections on basic cutting skills. Foods that grow in layers or have pits, cores, or seeds all require special handling. Onions, apples, tomatoes, and mangoes are examples of these ingredients. Bone-in cuts of meat, fish, and poultry also call for special cutting and carving techniques; read Meat & Poultry and Fish & Shellfish for more information about them.

There are many different ways to cut an onion. Select a method based on your specific needs. Some methods have the advantage of speed, important in volume cooking situations. Others produce very little waste, appropriate when there is no use for the trim. Still others are best when precise, even cuts are required.

Onions can bring tears to your eyes. Although there are many home-style remedies, the best advice is to use a very sharp knife so that the onion will be cut, not crushed.

To streamline your prep work, you can peel onions the day before you cut and cook them. Onions to be served raw should be cut at the last possible moment. As onions sit, they lose their flavor and develop a strong, unpleasant odor in a short time. If a portion of your sliced raw onions remains unused at the end of a shift, it should be added to a mirepoix, included in a stock or broth as it simmers, or, if there are no other uses, put in the compost bucket or thrown out.

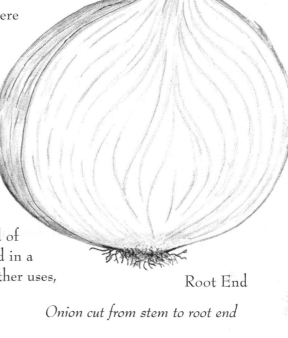

Stem End

Root End

Onion cut from stem to root end

Onions—continued ▶

Here is one method for peeling and cutting an onion.

a

1. Use a paring knife to remove the stem end of the onion. Peel off the skin and the underlying layer, if it contains brown spots (a). Trim the root end but leave it intact.

b

c

2. To dice or mince the onion, halve the onion lengthwise through the root (b).

3. Lay it cut-side down and make a series of evenly spaced, parallel, lengthwise cuts with the tip of a chef's knife, again leaving the root end intact (c).

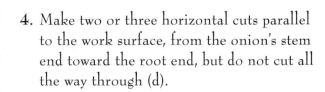

d

4. Make two or three horizontal cuts parallel to the work surface, from the onion's stem end toward the root end, but do not cut all the way through (d).

5. Make even crosswise cuts with a chef's knife all the way through from stem to root end. The closer the cuts in step 3 and in this step, the finer the dice will be (e, f).

e   *Fine dice*

f   *Medium dice*

A second method for peeling is especially good when you are going to cut and use the onion right away. (If you are peeling onions to use the next day, it is still best to leave them whole.)

1. Slice through the onion before trimming and peeling.

2. Pull away the skin from each half. The trimmed and peeled onion can be chopped, diced, or minced in the same manner as previously demonstrated.

Onions—continued ▶

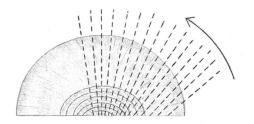

An alternative method for slicing or dicing an onion calls for a series of cuts to be made following the natural curve of the onion half, as shown in the accompanying illustration. Make a series of cuts evenly spaced over the curved surface of the onion. These cuts are sometimes referred to as *radial cuts*. ◀

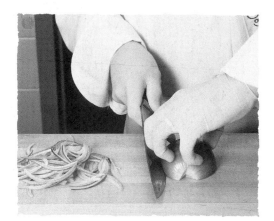

The stem of the onion can be left intact or removed depending on your final use. If the stem end is left intact, the onion can be minced or diced by making even crosswise cuts.

◀ If you are slicing onions into julienne, cut away the stem end by notching the onion and then making a series of cuts following its curve.

Slicing an onion for sandwiches or to make onion rings can easily be done with a chef's knife, a mando-line, or an electric slicer. ▶

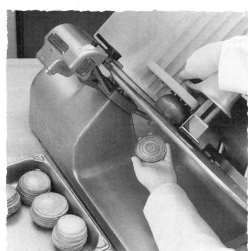

Shallots

Shallots are like onions in that they grow in layers. They also are like garlic in that they grow in cloves.

To mince shallots, first trim and peel the shallots as you would an onion. ◀

If the shallot has more than one clove, separate the cloves and make a series of perpendicular and horizon-tal cuts using the tip of your chef's knife, or a paring knife as shown. ▶

Scallions

To remove wilted outer layers from scallions, ramps, or small leeks, use your fingertips or clamp the layer you wish to remove between your thumb and the flat of a knife blade and pull the layer away (a utility knife is shown here). The next step, before slicing or mincing, is to trim away the root end.

By opening or closing the angle of your cut, you can cut the green tops of scallions on the diagonal, slice the light green portion, and mince the white portion.

Garlic

Chefs know that all members of the onion family have the best flavor and texture when you cut them by hand just before you cook them. Preparing garlic and shallots is part of the kitchen's daily mise en place.

Sometimes, however, you may have some uncooked minced garlic or shallots left over at the end of a shift. You can store them covered in oil under refrigeration for no more than twenty-four hours.

Special garlic peelers make it easy to peel the cloves; slicers can be used to shave paper-thin slices of garlic for sauces and sautés; and food processors or garlic presses are used by some to make puréed garlic. However, you can perform all these tasks with a sharp knife and a clean side towel, and have an easier cleanup and a better-quality product. Once this technique is mastered, it takes very little time to properly peel, slice, or mash garlic by hand in almost all situations except high-volume cooking, where using processors or purchasing minced garlic or shallots makes the most sense.

Note: Large quantities of garlic may be minced in a food processor. You may need to add a small amount of oil to the garlic as it is being puréed. The photo shows a garlic paste in a food processor next to a smaller quantity made with a knife.

To prepare quantities of garlic by hand:

1. Wrap an entire head of garlic in a side towel and press down on its top to break it into individual cloves (a).

a

2. If you press hard enough, the skin loosens on most of the cloves. The towel keeps the papery skin from flying around your work area. Use the heel of your hand or a closed fist to hit the clove (b).

3. The cloves should break cleanly away from the root end (c).

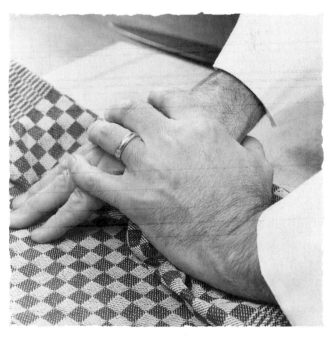

b

c

Garlic—continued ▶

d

4. To loosen the skin from each clove, crush it between the knife blade's flat side and the cutting board (d).

e

5. Peel off the skin and remove the root end and any brown spots (e). At some times of the year and under certain storage conditions, the garlic may begin to sprout. Split the clove in half and remove the core for the best flavor.

6. Lay the skinned cloves on the work surface and lay the flat of your blade over them. Using a motion similar to that for cracking the skin, hit the blade firmly with the heel of your hand or the fist. More force should be applied this time (f).

f

g

h

7. Chop the clove fairly fine, using a rocking motion (g).

8. Hold the knife nearly flat against the cutting surface angle and use the cutting edge to mash the garlic against the cutting board (h). Repeat this step until the garlic is mashed to a paste.

9. You may wish to sprinkle the garlic with salt before you mash it to a paste (i). The salt acts an abrasive, speeding the process of mashing the garlic and preventing the garlic from sticking to the knife blade.

i

Leeks grow in such a way that they are almost always filled with grit and sand. It is important to thoroughly clean leeks before cooking with them. To clean leeks, first rinse off all the surface dirt, paying special attention to the roots, where dirt clings.

1. Lay the rinsed leek on your cutting board and trim away the heavy green portion of the leaves with a chef's knife. By cutting on an angle, you can avoid losing the tender light-green portion of the leek (a). Reserve the dark-green portion of the leek to make bouquet garni or for another appropriate use.

2. Trim away most of the root end, then cut the leek lengthwise into halves, thirds, or quarters (b).

3. Rinse the leek under running water to remove any remaining grit or sand (c).

4. Now the leek can be cut into julienne (pictured) or other cuts as desired (d).

a

b

c

d

Clean the mushrooms just before you are ready to prepare them by rinsing quickly in cool water, just long enough to remove any dirt. Do not allow them to soak. (Some people feel that mushrooms should be cleaned by wiping with a soft cloth or brushing with a soft-bristled brush; this is not practical in a professional kitchen.) Let them drain and dry well before slicing or mincing. The stems of some mushrooms such as shiitakes, should be removed prior to slicing. White mushrooms, morels, cèpes, and portobello mushroom stems can usually be left intact although it is a good practice to cut a slice away from the stem end to trim away any dried or fibrous portions.

Mushrooms can be chopped or minced, cut into slices, julienne, or batonnet, and diced. The method shown here produces neat, precise cuts.

1. Holding the mushroom cap with your guiding hand, make slices through the cap and stem, if it has not been trimmed off. To cut a large amount efficiently, slice the mushrooms so that the slices are layered, as shown. The chef shown here is right-handed, so his work moves from right to left. Reverse the flow if you are left-handed.

2. Cut across the slices at the desired thickness to create juliennes.

3. Turn the juliennes so that they are parallel to the edge of the work surface. Make crosswise cuts to mince the mushrooms for use in duxelles or other applications.

The method for fluting mushrooms is shown on page 61.

Tomatoes are required in the preparation or finishing of many cooked and raw sauces and dishes. Peeled tomatoes are preferred for most refined dishes. Once peeled, tomatoes can be seeded and then chopped to make concassé or cut into neat dice or julienne.

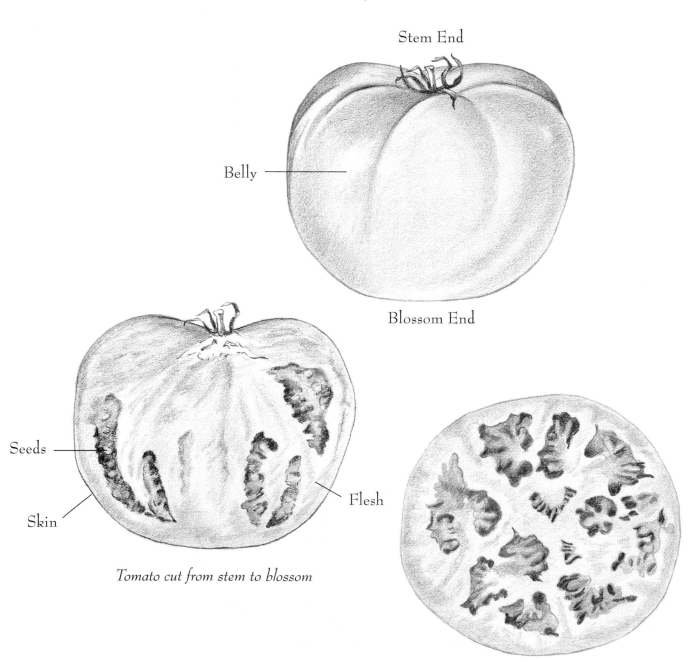

Stem End

Belly

Blossom End

Seeds

Skin

Flesh

Tomato cut from stem to blossom

Tomato cut across belly

The technique shown here for blanching and peeling tomatoes is also suitable for peaches, apricots, and some nuts.

1. Core the tomato, using the tip of your paring knife (a).

2. Score the blossom end of the tomato to make the skin easier to remove later on (b), if desired (some chefs skip this step).

a

b

3. Bring a pot of water to a rolling boil. Drop a few of the tomatoes into the water. Adding too many can drop the temperature of the water enough to slow the blanching process. After 10 to 30 seconds (depending on the tomatoes' age and ripeness), remove them with a slotted spoon, skimmer, or spider (c).

4. Immediately plunge them into ice water to prevent them from cooking any further (d).

c

d

Tomatoes—continued ▶

e

5. Use the tip of your paring knife to help pull away the skin. Catch the skin between your thumb and the flat side of the blade (e). If the tomato is ripe and was properly blanched, the skin should come away easily in a thin, translucent layer. If it does not, you may need to cut it from the tomato at the points where it adheres.

6. Halve the tomato crosswise at its widest point (f and g) and gently squeeze out the seeds. You may need to push out some of the seeds with your fingertip to remove all the seeds (h). Plum tomatoes are more easily seeded by cutting lengthwise.

f

g

h

Make parallel and horizontal cuts of the appropriate width and chop or cut into cubes or dice.

To cut peeled tomatoes into julienne, first halve or quarter the tomato (cutting from stem to blossom end) after you have removed the skin. Some chefs use a cutting motion similar to that used to peel a grapefruit (see page 89) to remove the tomato flesh from the seeds without halving or quartering the tomato first.

◀ Use the tip of your chef's knife to cut away any seeds and interior membranes, a process sometimes referred to as *filleting*.

Cut the flesh into julienne or other shapes as desired. ▼

To remove the skin and pit of an avocado, use the fingertips of your guiding hand to control the avocado, but don't press down too hard. Turn the avocado against the knife blade. The cut should pierce the skin and cut through the flesh up to the pit. ▶

Again using your fingertips to avoid bruising the avocado, twist the two halves apart.

Note: It can be difficult to remove the pit with your fingertips without mangling the flesh. You can "chop" the heel of your knife into the pit, then twist and pull it free from the flesh. To remove the pit from your knife safely, use the edge of your cutting board or the lip of a container to pry it free.

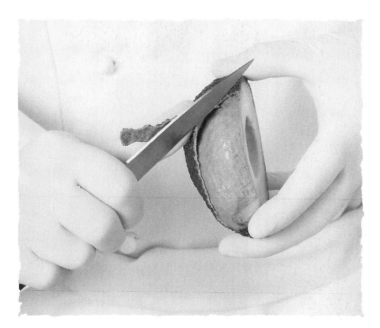

Catch the skin of the avocado between the ball of your thumb and the flat side of a blade (a utility knife is used here) and pull it free from the flesh. ◀

◄ Cut the avocado into wedges.

▼ To cube the avocado,
cut crosswise through the wedges.

An alternative method shown here for peeling and dicing
an avocado is particularly effective if the avocado is
extremely ripe.

Once the avocado is halved and the pit removed, as
described above, use the side of a kitchen spoon to scoop
out the flesh. ▶

To dice an avocado while it is still in the skin, use the tip of a
knife to score the flesh into dice of the desired size. Using a
kitchen spoon,
scoop through the
flesh, working in
layers, to create
neat dice. ▶

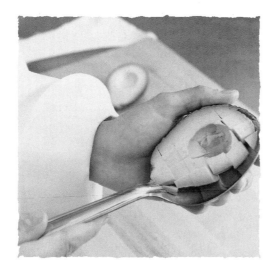

Peppers

Peppers and chiles are pods with a cluster of seeds attached to the stem end and the fleshy ribs. Hot peppers (chiles) have oils that can irritate your skin. We suggest that you wear disposable gloves when working with chiles. Whether you wear gloves or not, don't touch your eyes or other sensitive areas. Wash your hands thoroughly in plenty of warm soapy water to remove any residue from the chile.

This cutting method creates the least trim loss.

◄ Cut through the pepper from stem to blossom end. You may continue to cut it into quarters, especially if the pepper is large.

Use the tip of your paring knife to cut away the stem and the seeds. This removes the least amount of usable pepper. ▼

An alternative, when you wish to cut a pepper into very neat dice or julienne, is to slice through the stem and blossom ends. This removes the shoulders of the pepper and the pointed tail; the trim can be saved for other use. Make a slice through the flesh and lay the pepper out flat. Hold the pepper with your guiding hand so that it is stable. Hold the knife blade parallel to the work surface and cut away the membranes and the seeds in one motion. ▶

To produce peeled peppers that have not been roasted, repeat the same cutting motion used above to cut the tough skin away from the pepper's flesh. Peeled peppers prepared this way have a fresh flavor, a more appealing texture, and are better able to absorb flavors from marinades and dressings. ▼

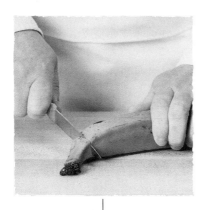

Plantains look like bananas, but have a tougher skin. They are usually served as a side dish and are typically fried.

1. Cut away the stem end of the plantain with a paring knife.

2. Score the outer peel by cutting along the ridges.

3. Pull away the peel to expose the flesh.

4. Cut the flesh into rondelles or long strips to prepare for frying.

Zucchini may be cut into a variety of shapes. The methods for cutting rondelles, ripple cuts, and ribbons can be found on pages 49 to 50. Two approaches for making very precise julienne, by hand or on a mandoline, are shown here.

To cut by hand, first cut the zucchini into 2-inch lengths. Make parallel slices to the desired thickness.

Stack the slices and make parallel slices to produce even julienne or batonnet of the required dimensions.

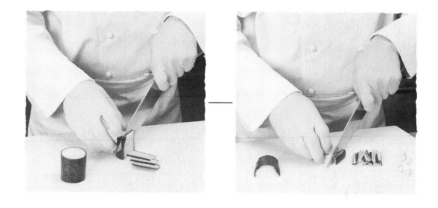

To cut julienne on a mandoline, cut the zucchini into sections of your desired finished length. Pass the zucchini over the fine opening of the cutting blades on your mandoline. Give the zucchini a quarter turn when the seeds are exposed and continue cutting from each face until only the seeds remain. ▶

a

b

The cutting techniques demonstrated here on an apple are also appropriate for fruits such as pears and vegetables such as soft-skinned squashes.

1. Use the tip of a paring knife to remove the stem and blossoms ends (a and b). If you use an apple corer instead, the seeds are removed in the same motion.

2. Use a paring knife to cut away the skin. Use your guiding hand to hold and turn the apple against the blade. The thumb of the hand holding the peeler or knife should also be placed against the apple to keep it stable and prevent slipping (c). The peeling should be as thin as possible to avoid trim loss. (A peeler could also be used.)

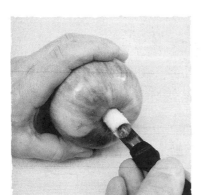

An apple corer can be used to remove stem and blossom ends, and seeds.

c

d

e

3. Once the peel is removed, halve the apple from top to bottom (d) and cut it into quarters.

4. Make a cut that scoops out the seeds (e). You may find it best to remove the core in two cuts. Work from the stem end, angling your cut to the midpoint of the core, where it is deepest. Make a second cut from the opposite direction. Cutting a notch in this way removes the core, leaving behind as much apple flesh as possible.

5. Continue to cut the apple into wedges or slices of the desired thickness (f). If you wish, the wedges can be cross-cut to make chopped or diced apples (g).

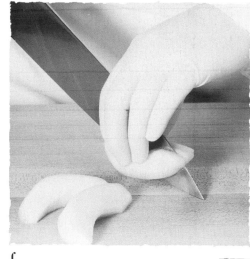

f

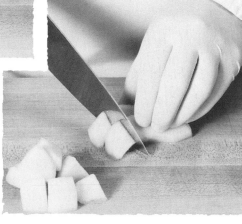

g

Apples—continued ▶

You can cut apples into very even slices with maximum yield by working with their natural shape and structure. A utility knife or mandoline (shown here) can be used.

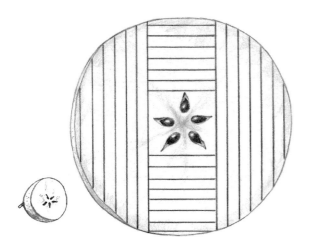

Cross-section of apple, showing slicing lines and core location.

1. Peel the apple if desired or necessary. Set the mandoline's slicing blade to make slices of the desired thickness. Holding the apple carefully, with fingertips well out of the blade's way, start to remove slices from one side of the apple (a). When you reach the core, turn the apple over and remove slices from the opposite side.

2. When the slices have been removed from both of the wider sides, slice the apple flesh from the narrow sides of the apple (b).

Use less attractive slices to fill the tart, and finish with a spiral of uniform slices, as shown.

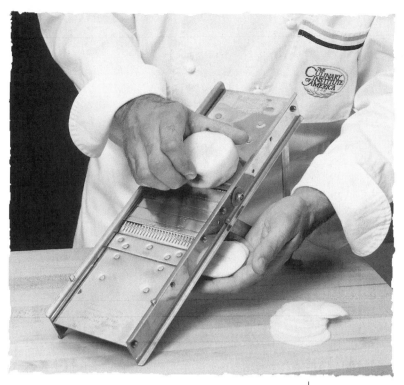

a

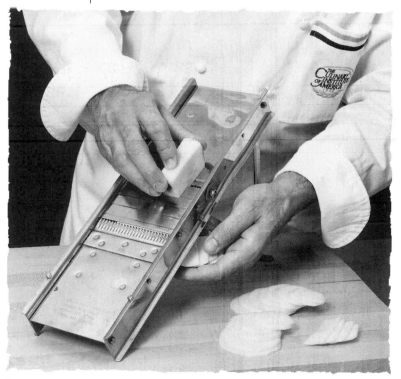

b

Citrus Fruit

Citrus zest is the outer portion of a citrus fruit's peel or rind. It is used to add color, texture, and flavor to various dishes. The zest includes only the skin's brightly colored part, which contains much of the fruit's flavorful and aromatic volatile oils. It does not include the underlying white pith, which has a bitter taste.

Zest is often blanched before it is used in a dish to remove any unpleasant bitter flavor. The blanching process also removes any chemical residue from the surface. To blanch zest, cook it briefly in simmering water, then drain. Repeat as often as necessary; generally, two to three blanchings is best. If a sweetened zest is desired, add sugar to the blanching water.

You can use a variety of tools to produce zest; for example, the fine openings on a box grater yield grated zest. You also can cut zest using the tools shown here.

Use a paring knife or peeler to cut away very thin strips of zest. Use a chef's knife to shred or mince the zest. ▶

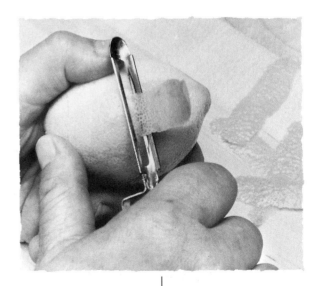

Alternately, use a citrus zester to remove only the peel's colored portion. ▼

Citrus suprêmes, also called sections or segments, are made by cutting the flesh away from all the connective membranes of the fruit. The method for making grapefruit suprêmes is as follows:

1. Cut away both ends of the fruit to make it easy to control (a).

2. Use the midsection of the cutting edge (a chef's knife is pictured, but a utility or paring knife is best for smaller fruits), cut the skin and the pith completely away (b). Your knife should follow the natural curve of the fruit. A little flesh will adhere to the skin, but it should not be a very large amount.

3. Holding the fruit in your hand, slice next to the connective membrane on one side of each citrus segment (c).

4. Twist the knife to turn the direction of your cut, and use a scooping motion to cut out the citrus flesh (d).

a

b

c

d

a

Melons can be peeled before or after cutting into wedges, slices, or cubes. You may wish to remove the entire rind before halving the melon and removing the seeds to streamline production of fruit plates and salads. In other cases, you may prefer to leave the rind on. In that case, the melon is halved and the seeds removed. It is generally easier to prepare melon balls if the skin is left in place after halving the melon and removing the seeds.

1. Use your chef's knife to cut a slice from both ends of the melon to stabilize it on the cutting surface (a).

2. Use a utility or chef's knife to peel the skin away. Your blade should follow the curve of the melon (b).

3. Cut the melon in half and scoop out the seeds (c).

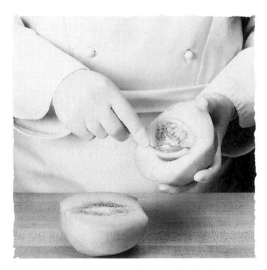

c

b

d

4. The melon can now be cut into even slices (d). These slices can be used to make neat cubes or dice (e).

e

Melons—continued ▶

The peeled and seeded melon can be cut into wedges. To make very regular size chunks, you may wish to trim the tapered ends of each wedge before cutting them into chunks.

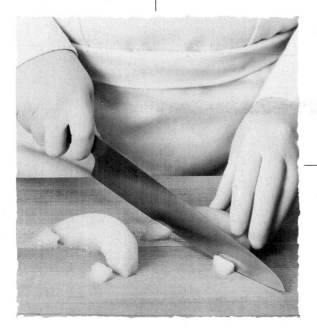

◀ An alternative method for cutting melon for salads is shown here. Leave the rind intact and cut through the melon from blossom end to stem end to make wedges or through the belly to make melon balls (as on page 60) or to leave whole for presentation as a melon half. Scoop out the seeds with a spoon and cut into wedges.

If desired, the flesh can be scored by cutting through it up to but not through the rind. Make a horizontal cut to slice the melon chunks away from the rind. ▼

a

b

c

To get the best yield from a pineapple, be sure to select the trimming and peeling method appropriate for your final use. Two methods are illustrated here.

1. Slice away the pineapple top with a chef's knife and cut a slice from the base (a).

2. Use your chef's knife to peel the pineapple, making sure that your cuts are deep enough to remove the eyes but not so deep that a great deal of edible flesh is removed (b).

3. To make neat dice or cubes, slice the pineapple evenly at the desired thickness until you reach the core on the first side (c). Turn the pineapple and make slices from the opposite side as well as from both ends (d). This technique is similar to that used to slice apples for apple tart (see pages 86–87).

d

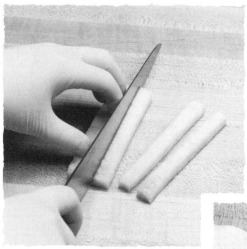

e

4. The slices can be cut into neat julienne (e) or batonnet or diced to the appropriate size (f).

5. To prepare wedges, cut the peeled pineapple into halves, quarters, or eighths, depending upon the pineapple's size or your specific needs. Cut out the core (g). Slice the pineapple if desired (h).

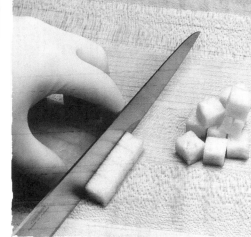

f

g

h

Pineapples—continued ▶

There is an alternative method for peeling a pineapple and making pineapple rings.

Cut a slice from the pineapple's base. You may wish to leave the pineapple top intact to make maneuvering easier. It also makes an attractive display piece.

Trim away the skin in the same manner as shown on the preceding pages, removing only the peel. There will still be eyes left in the flesh. Once the peel is removed, you can see the spiral pattern of the eyes. Using a chef's knife or a utility knife, cut the eyes out by making a V-shaped cut that follows their pattern. ▶

To prepare pineapple rings, slice a peeled pineapple crosswise and use a round cutter to remove the core. Or, you may prefer to use a large cutter, similar to an apple corer, to remove the core from the entire pineapple before cutting it into rings. ▼

Trimmed pineapple before cutting.

A mango has a wide, flat seed in the center of the flesh.

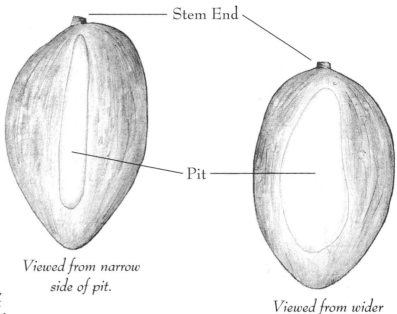

Stem End

Pit

Viewed from narrow side of pit.

Viewed from wider side of pit.

1. To prepare a mango for peeling, slicing, and dicing, first cut a slice from the broader end and remove the peel in the same way that you would from a pineapple or a melon (a).

2. Slice the mango flesh away from the pit by making a cut slightly off center, working from the stem end to the tip of the mango. If you cut from the stem end to the pointed end of the mango, the flesh comes away from the pit more easily. Your knife should scrape against the pit (b).

a

b

Mangoes—continued ▶

c

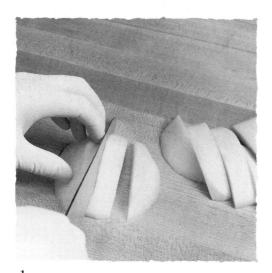

d

3. Cut a slice from the other side of the pit, cutting as close to the pit as possible for the best yield. Cut the remaining flesh from the two narrow sides as shown, following the curve of the pit (c).

4. You can now slice (d) or cube (e) the mango, as desired.

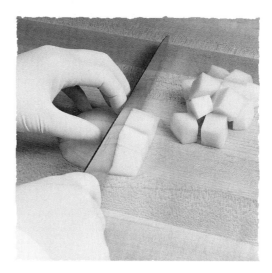

e

Another option for working with a mango eliminates the need to cut away the peel.

1. Cut the flesh on one of the wider sides from the pit, cutting as closely as possible to the pit and following its natural curve as closely as possible.

2. Use the tip of a paring knife or a utility knife to score the flesh in a crosshatch pattern. The tip of your knife should not cut through the skin.

3. Turn the mango half inside out; it will look like a hedgehog. You can slice the cubes away from the flesh now, or present the fruit as is on a fruit plate.

Meat & Poultry

The difference between butchering and fabricating meats is subtle. In the broad view, however, butchering means cutting an entire animal into large cuts known as primal cuts. Subsequent cuts are made to fabricate the primal into a variety of smaller cuts (known as subprimals or wholesale cuts). Fabrication, though it involves the meat-cutting techniques used in the butcher shop, is essentially the fine-tuning of an item purchased from a butcher or meat purveyor to produce the menu cuts familiar to most chefs and restaurant patrons.

Preparing your own meat and poultry menu cuts helps to keep food costs down, as long as trim loss is kept to a minimum. Use wholesome trim to prepare a variety of ground meat items, including burgers, sausages, and pâtés. Poultry wings can be used to make bar food and appetizers. Use bones to prepare stocks or broths, lessening your dependence on purchased bones and prepared bases.

The tenderloin is one of the most expensive cuts of meat, so care should be taken to leave the meat as intact as possible. Use a very sharp boning knife and pay close attention to your work.

The technique shown with a beef tenderloin can also be used to trim veal, pork, game, and lamb tenderloins, as well as other cuts of meat with silverskin, including top rounds of beef and veal, loin cuts of venison and other large game, and so forth.

1. Lift and pull away the fat covering, if you have purchased an untrimmed tenderloin. This fat pulls away easily, and the blade of the boning knife is used to steady the tenderloin as the fat cover is pulled away (a).

2. Pull and cut away the strip of fat and meat known as the *chain* (b and c). This trim can be further cleaned of excess fat and used in a variety of preparations, including stocks, broths, sauces, soups, and ground meat items.

a

b

Tenderloin—continued ▶

c

3. When the fat cover is removed, you can see a tough membrane covering the smooth side of the tenderloin. This membrane is known as the silverskin. The silverskin must be removed before cooking. If it is left in place, it shrinks when exposed to heat and causes uneven cooking and spoils the appearance of the dish. Position the tenderloin so that the tail is to the left, if you are right-handed, or to the right, if you are left-handed.

4. Work the tip of a boning knife under the silverskin; hold the end of the silverskin tight against the meat with your guiding hand and glide the knife blade just underneath (d). Angle the blade upward slightly so that only the silverskin is cut away.

d

Menu Cuts

The following terms are associated primarily with the beef tenderloin:

Chateaubriand: Chateaubriand is a thick cut (weighing approximately 10 ounces and meant to serve 2) taken from the middle of the fillet. Traditionally grilled then served with a sauce and potatoes. The term refers more properly to a specific recipe than a cut from the tenderloin.

Tournedos: Tournedos are cut from the thinner end of the tenderloin. They are rounder that the filet mignon cut, and are usually cut into pieces weighing 4 to 5 ounces.

Filet mignon: Filet mignon are cuts from the end of the tenderloin nearest the end that are too small to be properly termed *tournedos*. The term *mignon* indicates something small, or delicate—a small delicate cut from the tenderloin. Filet mignon are generally cut into pieces weighing 5 to 6 ounces.

Cuts produced from the loin or tenderloin of other animals are generally referred to as follows:

Medallions: Medallions are cut in the same manner as beef tournedos. The weight of the medallions will vary, depending upon the size of the loin or tenderloin being fabricated.

Noisettes: Noisettes are cut from the tenderloin or loin; generally smaller than a medallion.

Shaping a Medallion

To make medallions and similar menu cuts of meat, slice a boneless top round, loin or tenderloin (beef, veal, lamb, game, or pork) into portions of the size you require.

Once the medallion or other cut is prepared, you may shape it by wrapping it in dampened cheesecloth and shaping it into a compact, uniform shape. This is done to encourage even and uniform cooking as well as to give the meat a more attractive look.

1. Cut the boneless meat into pieces of equal weight. The tenderloin shown here has been cut into 6-ounce pieces. To make each piece a uniform size, cut cheesecloth in a square large enough to easily wrap the meat portion.

2. Gather the cheesecloth together and twist to tighten it around the meat (a). As you twist the cloth with one hand, press down firmly on the meat with even, moderate pressure (b). Remove the cheesecloth once the desired shape is achieved.

3. The shaped medallion (c, foreground) can now be wrapped with bacon, if desired; it is ready for grilling or sautéing.

a

b

c

Chops and steaks are made from bone-in cuts such as rib and loin. A saw is necessary to cut through bones. Large bones can be difficult to saw through, but the rib and loin of pork, lamb, venison, and beef have more manageable bones.

1. First, cut through the chine bone using a handsaw (a). The chine bone should be completely severed but not cut away from the meat.

2. Use your guiding hand to hold the chine bone away from the meat. Work with the tip of your boning knife to make smooth strokes along the feather bones, cutting the meat cleanly away from them (b).

3. Continue cutting until the chine bone and the feather bones are completely released from the meat (c).

4. Cut between each rib bone with a scimitar (d) or chef's knife to make individual chops. The cut should be very smooth to create a smooth surface on the chops. Once cut, the meaty portion of rib chops from pork, lamb, and venison can be shaped using the technique demonstrated with a beef tenderloin on page 103.

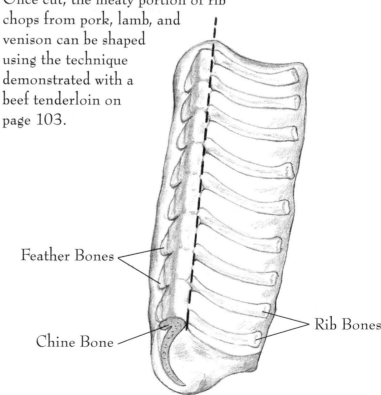

Feather Bones

Chine Bone

Rib Bones

Dotted line shows cutting line for saw

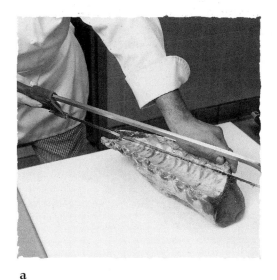

a

b

c

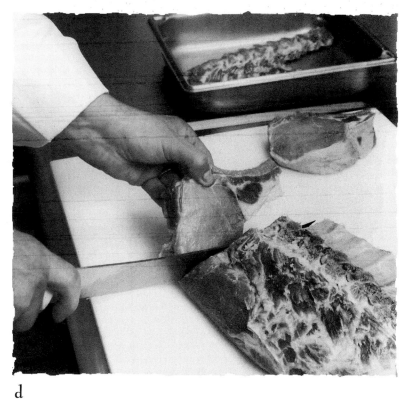

d

Although this procedure looks difficult, you can do it successfully by following the steps shown here. A leg of lamb has the same basic structure as a veal or venison leg. You can use the same general procedure to bone those cuts.

1. First, remove the flank, a portion of muscle that is loosely attached to the underside of the leg (a).

2. Cut into the fat at the point closest to the lean muscle tissue. This incision makes it easier to pull the fat cover away from the fell (b). Make cuts to separate the fell from the fat layer below it, rolling the leg as you work.

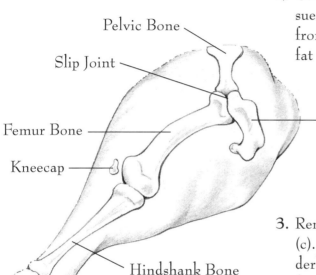

Pelvic Bone

Slip Joint

Femur Bone

Kneecap

Tailbone

Hindshank Bone

3. Remove the fat and blood vessels from the butt tenderloin (c). Use the tip of your boning knife to cut the butt tenderloin away from the tail, but do not sever it completely from the rest of the leg meat.

4. Remove the tailbone from the pelvic bone. The cut is made at the slip joint (d).

5. Using the overhand grip to hold the boning knife, work the tip of the knife around the pelvic bone (e).

6. When the meat is freed from the pelvic bone, lift the bone up and away from the leg meat and cut it cleanly away from the meat (f).

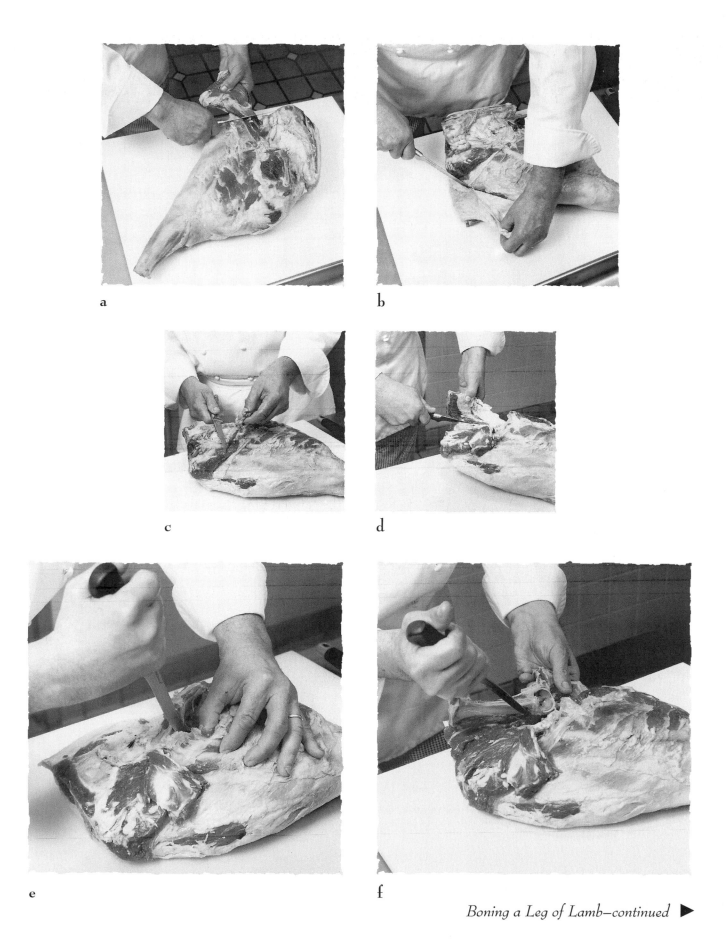

a

b

c

d

e

f

Boning a Leg of Lamb—continued ▶

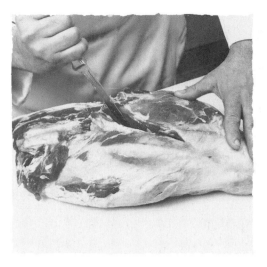

g

7. Turn the leg so that the ball joint of the femur bone is uppermost. Look for a seam of fat that runs parallel and close to the top of the femur. Make a cut into the meat, following the seam, until you reach the femur (g).

8. Use the tip of your boning knife to cut the meat cleanly away from the femur. The tip should touch the bone each time you make a stroke; this keeps trim loss to a minimum. Note how little meat is left clinging to the bone (h).

9. As you continue to expose the femur, the hind-shank bone becomes visible (i).

i

h

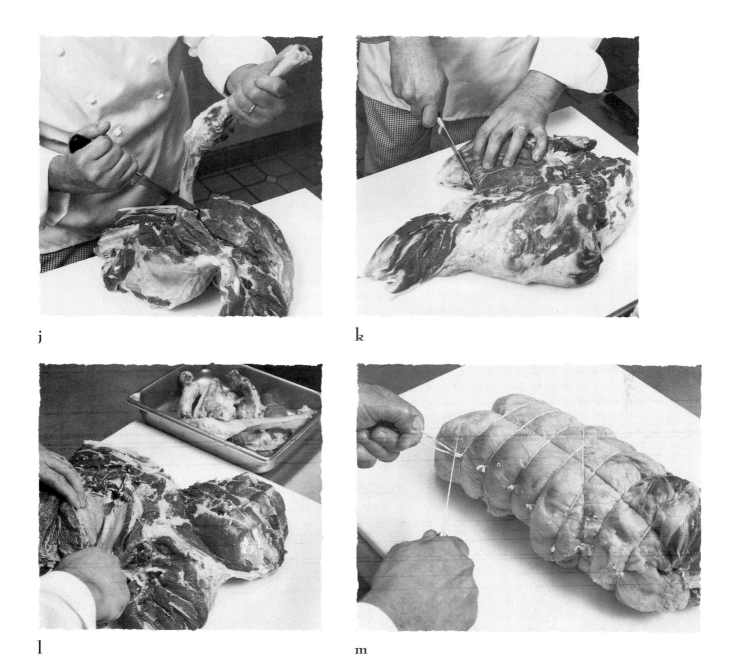

j

k

l

m

10. Using the same cutting action as you did to expose the femur, cut the meat away from the hindshank bone. Lift the femur and the hind shankbone up and away from the meat as you continue to cut them completely free from the meat (j).

11. Remove the kneecap, or *patella* (k).

12. Use your fingers to check for a large fat deposit in the leg of meat (l). Cut it away.

13. The roast is now ready to roll and tie (m); it may be prepared for other presentations as well.

Rabbit is a relatively lean, mildly flavored meat that can be used for a number of preparations. The loin and rib sections tend to be drier than the legs, in much the same way that the chicken breast can be drier than the legs. By first removing the legs and shoulder, two different cooking methods can be applied to one rabbit—moist heat for the legs, dry heat for the loin—to achieve the most satisfactory results.

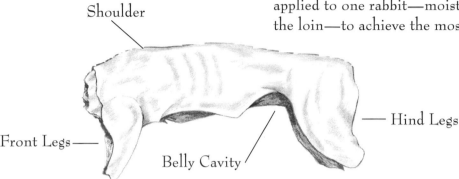

Shoulder

Front Legs

Belly Cavity

Hind Legs

1. Spread open the belly cavity of the rabbit and pull out the kidney and liver. Sever any membrane attaching the liver to the cavity (a). The liver should be reserved for another use.

2. Remove the hind legs by cutting through the joint (b); cut through the meat to separate the hind leg from the loin.

3. To separate the front legs and shoulder from the rest of the body, pull the leg away from the body and cut through the joint (c).

4. Trim the loin by cutting away the hind and front portions to produce the saddle (d and e).

◄ A fully disjointed rabbit is pictured here, including saddle, foreleg and shoulder sections, hind legs, liver, kidneys, and usable trim. The trim may be used to make a game stock, if desired.

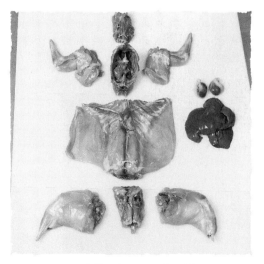

The fully disjointed rabbit.

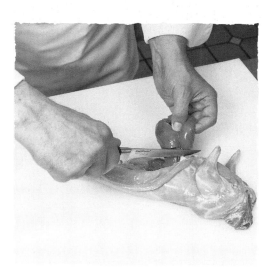

a

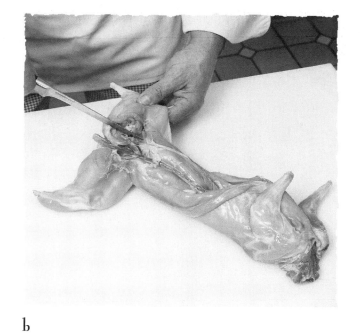

b

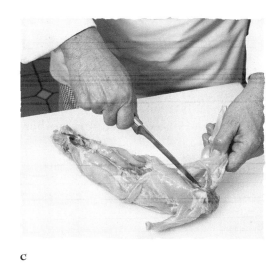

c

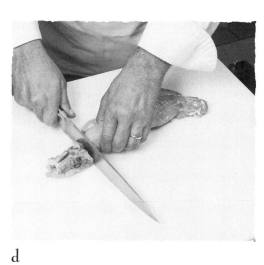

d

e

Chicken and other young birds are easy to cut up in the kitchen, and the skills necessary to halve and quarter a whole bird, as well as make a suprême, should be second nature to a professional chef. The younger the bird, the easier it is to cut up, as its bones are not completely hardened. The size and breed of the bird has some bearing on how easy or difficult it is to fabricate; chickens are generally far more simple to cut up, for example, than are pheasant. The tendons and ligaments in chickens are less well developed than in game birds.

A suprême is a semiboneless poultry breast, usually from a chicken, pheasant, partridge, or duck. It is so named because it is the best (supreme) chicken portion. One wing joint, often frenched, is left attached to the breast meat. If the skin is removed from the suprême, the cut may be referred to as a *côtelette*. Suprêmes may be sautéed, poached, or grilled.

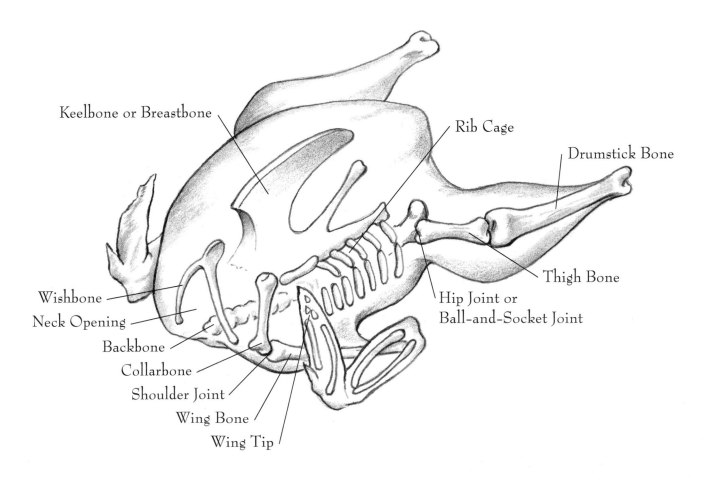

Keelbone or Breastbone

Rib Cage

Drumstick Bone

Thigh Bone

Hip Joint or
Ball-and-Socket Joint

Wishbone

Neck Opening

Backbone

Collarbone

Shoulder Joint

Wing Bone

Wing Tip

Several methods are used to prepare a suprême. Two methods are illustrated here. The first method shows two cutting techniques used to prepare a chicken for trussing (removing wing tips) or disjointing (removing the legs).

1. Use the tip of your boning knife to make a cut that circles around the second joint of the wing bone (a). Make sure that you cut through the web skin as well.

2. Bend the wing bone at the second joint to snap it. Continue to cut through the joint until the first two joints are removed (b).

3. Cut through the skin between the thigh and the leg (c).

4. Bend the leg backward, away from the body, to expose the ball-and-socket joint (d).

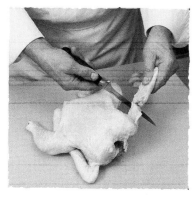

a

b

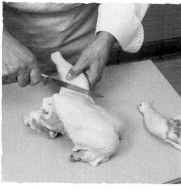

c

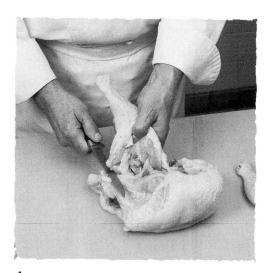

d

Poultry–continued ▶

5. Make a cut that runs along the backbone up to the ball-and-socket joint (e).

6. Hold the chicken stable with the heel of your knife and pull the leg away from the body firmly and evenly (f). This removes the leg and the oyster cleanly from the backbone structure.

7. With the breast facing up, cut along either side of the keel bone with the knife (g). Use your guiding hand to steady the bird.

8. Remove the breast meat from the ribcage (h). The cuts should be delicate; use the tip of your knife to free the meat, running the tip along the bones for the best yield.

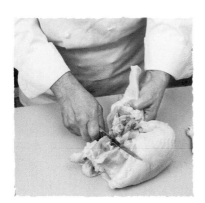

e

f

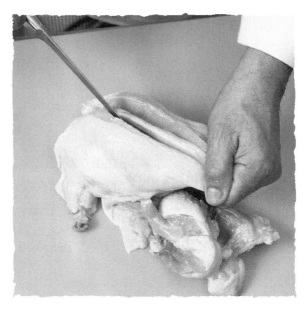

g

h

A second method for preparing a suprême calls for the back-bone to be removed before cutting the breast portions away from the rib bones, a technique also used to halve whole chickens.

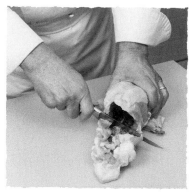

a

1. Remove the wing tips and legs from the bird as described in steps 1 through 3 (page 113).

2. Cut through the connective tissue holding the breast to the backbone (a). This cut should not sever the backbone.

3. Hold the chicken's tail with your guiding hand and cut from the tail to the neck opening on either side of the backbone (b). Pull upward slightly as you cut down; make sure to exert enough pressure to cut through the rib bones.

4. Lay out the whole breast, with the bones facing up. Use the tip of your boning knife to cut through the white cartilage at the very top of the keel bone (c).

5. Open out the breast as you would a book (d). This bending action should expose the keel bone.

b

c

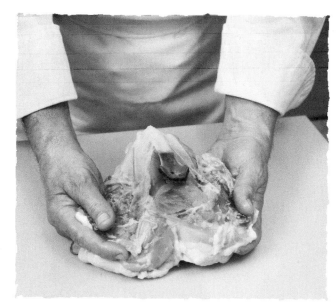

d

Poultry—continued ▶

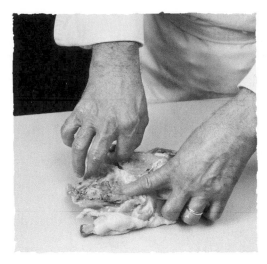

e

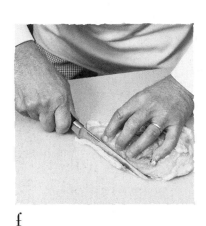

f

6. Grab the keel bone firmly and pull it and the attached cartilage away from the breast meat (e). If the bird is young, they will come out in one piece. If the bird is older, the cartilage may break away from the keel bone. Be sure to remove the entire structure.

7. Cut through the breast into two portions. Trim away any remaining cartilage or connective tissue (f).

8. Hold the breast as shown and carefully cut the bones away from the meat (g). Cut down to the wing joint, but be careful not to cut the wing bone away from the suprême.

9. Carefully cut away the bones at the wing joint (h). The suprême should be trimmed and frenched as shown on the facing page.

g

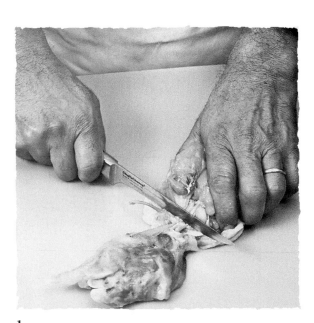

h

◀ Trim away the excess fat and skin from the breast.

Use the blade edge to scrape the meat on the wing bone to expose the bone completely. This is known as *frenching* the bone. ▶

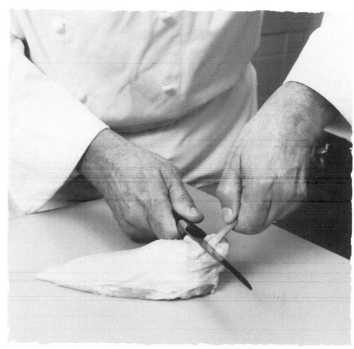

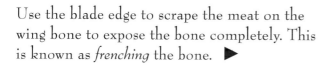

The finished suprêmes.

Poultry—continued ▶

Halving and Quartering Poultry

Chicken and other birds may also be halved before or after cooking. The process is the same in both cases.

1. Remove the backbone as described in steps 2 and 3 of the second method for preparing a suprême (page 115).

2. Remove the keel bone as described in steps 4 and 5 of the second method for preparing a suprême (page 115).

3. Cut the chicken into halves by making a cut down the center of the breast to divide the bird in half.

4. Separate the leg and thigh from the breast and wing by cutting through the skin just above where the breast and thigh meet.

The chicken is now quartered. The pieces may be grilled, baked, or stewed, as desired.

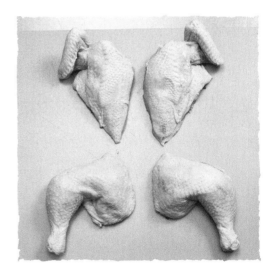

Even after the food is properly roasted, your work is not complete. The food must be carved correctly to make the most of the item. Most meats, poultry, and fish are cut into serving-sized portions before they are cooked, although occasionally it is more appropriate to prepare a large roast or an entire bird. The carving techniques shown here are suitable for use in the kitchen.

Be sure to wear clean food-handler's gloves when you work with cooked foods to keep them safe. (For additional important information about safe food handling and gloves, see page 41.)

Rib Roast

This carving method, illustrated with a rib roast here, could also be used for a rack of veal or lamb.

1. Lay the rib roast on its side. Using a sharp meat slicer, make a horizontal cut from the outer edge up to the rib bones. Use your kitchen fork to hold the meat steady as you cut. The cut should be parallel to the cutting surface.

2. Hold your knife so that you can make a cut along the bones to free the slice of meat. This cut is done with the knife held vertically rather than horizontally.

Ham

Once a ham is properly roasted, allow it to rest before carving. The same basic procedure could be followed for other leg cuts (leg of lamb or venison, for example). Two major muscles are attached to the leg, known variously as the *inner* and *outer rounds* or the *top* and *bottom rounds*. The top (or outer) round is larger and has a more pronounced curve.

Remember to reserve the ham bone as well as any wholesome trim for other uses. The bone can be used to flavor bean or lentil soups and stews and to make a rich broth. Lean trim can be used to make garnishes for soups, sauces, omelets, braises, and forcemeat items such as pâtés and terrines, as well as to prepare spreads, meat salads, and mousses. The method for carving a ham is as follows:

1. Holding the ham steady, use a slicer to trim away the excess fat cover (a). The amount you trim away is a matter of preference, but most diners today favor a clean trim.

2. Stand the ham on end, with the sirloin end resting on the board. Hold the shank end with your guiding hand to keep the ham stable. Using your slicer, make a cut into the lean meat just below the stifle joint on the shank end (b). The cut should follow the natural curve of the femur. Cut close to the bone for the best yield.

3. Cut around the ball-and-socket joint (c). This first cut will not cut the meat completely away from the bone.

4. Repeat the same steps described in steps 1 through 3 to cut the meat from the second side of the bone. This cut should release the top round from the bone. Note that the meat appears to have a V-shaped notch where it is cut away from the bone (d).

5. Cut away the meat (bottom round) from the back of the femur (e). Keep the pieces of meat as intact as possible.

6. Carve the ham into slices with a ham or meat slicer (f). The ham could also be sliced on an electric meat slicer, if you are preparing a large quantity for a banquet or other volume feeding situation.

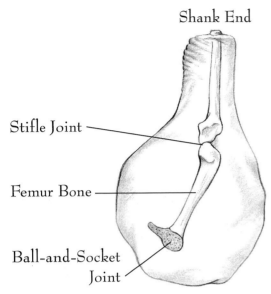

Shank End

Stifle Joint

Femur Bone

Ball-and-Socket Joint

Sirloin End

a

b

c

d

e

f

Duck

When your guest orders roast duck, this presentation is the most user-friendly. The duck is halved and the bones removed so that the leg portion has only the drumstick bone and the breast portion a single wing bone. They are nestled together so that the boneless breast and thigh meat overlap. Your guest can simply cut into the meat without having to work around bones.

1. Cut the legs away from body at the point where leg meets breast (a). As you pull away the leg, you will reach the ball-and-socket joint.

2. Removing the thigh bone from the leg by simultaneously pulling up the bone and cutting the meat away with the tip of your boning knife (b).

a

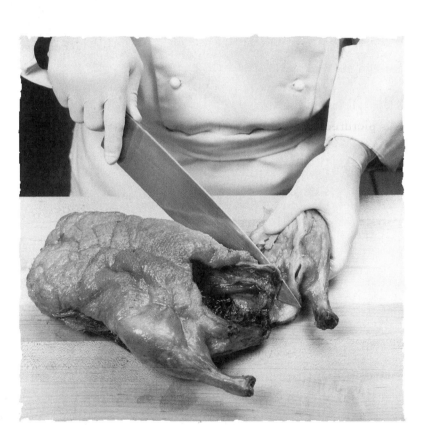

b

c

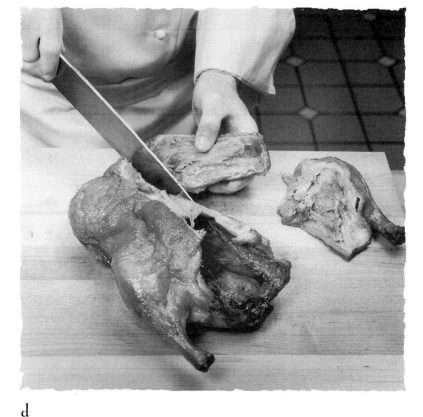

3. Carve the breast away from the ribcage with little trim loss by making your blade edge run as close to the bones as possible (c and d).

d

4. Pull the thigh bone up and away from the thigh meat. Use your knife as pictured to separate the bone at the leg joint (e).

5. Nest the leg and breast portions for presentation (f). The leg portion is positioned on the bottom and the breast portion overlapped, with the drumstick bone and the wing bone on opposite sides.

e

f

Turkey

Carving a turkey in the kitchen permits you greater control over carving loss. The turkey portions can be prepared and held in hotel pans or sheet pans to simplify banquet service, if desired.

1. Roasted foods of all sorts are more flavorful and easier to carve if they are allowed to rest after roasting. This turkey is resting prior to carving while the chef prepares a pan-gravy (a).

2. Cut away the first two segments of the turkey wings (b). (The meat can be removed from the segment left attached to the breast so that you can grip it more easily.)

3. Cut the legs away from the breast by cutting through the crease where the thigh meets the breast and severing the ball-and-socket joint (c). Pull the leg away from the body as you work to make it easier to reach the joint.

4. Remove the breast meat by making a cut just to one side of the ridge running the length of the breast (d).

5. Continue carving the meat from the rib bones. Pull the breast away from the carcass as you work. Very little meat should be left clinging to the bones (e and f). Carve the boneless portion of the breast into slices.

6. Remove the thigh bone from the turkey leg was done for duck (page 122, step 2). Hold onto the drumstick bone to steady the thigh as you carve the boneless meat into slices (g). To hold for banquet service, arrange slices of dark and white meat as shown.

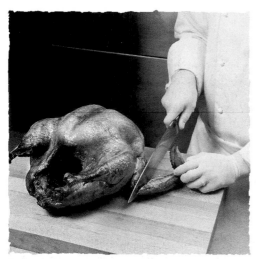

a

b

c

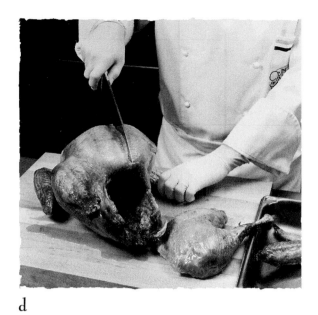

d

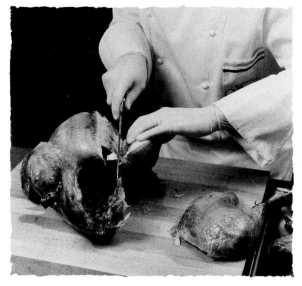

e

f

g

Fish & Shellfish

F ish and shellfish are popular on most menus and demand continues to grow. If you can cut your own fish, you can be assured of good quality, portion sizes that meet your specifications, and a lower overall food cost. Edible trim can be used in a variety of applications, such as fillings and stuffings, soups, sauces, and salads. Bones and shells can be used to make soups and stocks.

The fish and shellfish fabrication techniques shown here include filleting and portioning fish, peeling and deveining shrimp, working with raw and cooked lobster, and opening clams and oysters.

Head Gill Plates Backbone

Pin Bones Belly Bones Tail

Fillets are one of the most common ways to fabricate a fish. These boneless and (usually) skinless fish pieces can be sautéed, grilled, baked, formed into paupiettes, or cut into tranches or goujonettes. The technique for preparing skinless salmon fillets and cutting them into portions is illustrated here.

a

1. Lay the salmon on a cutting board with the backbone parallel to the work surface and the head on the same side as the hand holding your knife.

2. Cut behind the head and gill plates. Angle the knife so that the cutting motion is down and away from the body (a). This cut does not cut the head of the salmon away from the body.

3. Without removing the knife, turn it so that the cutting edge is pointing toward the tail of the fish. Position the knife so that the handle is lower than the tip of the blade. This improves the yield by keeping the knife's edge aimed at the bones rather than the salmon flesh.

4. Run the blade down the length of the salmon, cutting against the backbone (b). Avoid sawing the knife back and forth. If you cut evenly and smoothly, you should actually split the tail (c). Once the fillet is freed from the bones, lay it skin side down on the work surface or in a hotel pan. Lift the fillet with both hands to keep it intact.

b

c

Salmon—continued ▶

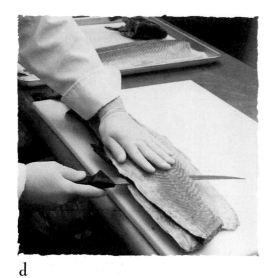

d

e

f

5. Without turning the fish over, insert the blade just underneath the backbone. Lay your guiding hand flat on top of the bone structure to keep the salmon stable. Hold the knife parallel to the cutting surface (d). Using the same smooth cutting motion, run the blade the entire length of the fillet.

6. Angle the cutting edge upward very slightly so that you are cutting against the bone to increase the usable yield on the second fillet (e).

7. Remove the belly bones by making smooth strokes just underneath them to cut them cleanly away (f).

8. Cut away the remnants of the backbone by running the blade just underneath its line, lifting it up and away from the fillet as you cut (g).

9. To remove the skin, lay the fillet parallel to the edge of your cutting surface, with the tail to the left if you are right-handed and to the right if you are left-handed. Hold the tail firmly with your guiding hand and carefully insert the knife between the skin and the flesh. Holding the knife so that the cutting edge is cutting against the skin, pull the skin taut with your guiding hand as you cut the salmon fillet free from the skin (h). The motion should be relatively smooth, with a very slight sawing motion.

g

h

10. The pin bones should be removed at this point. They can be located by running a fingertip over the fillet. Use pliers or tweezers to pull out the bones (i). Pull them out in the direction of the head of the fillet (working with the grain) to avoid ripping the flesh.

i

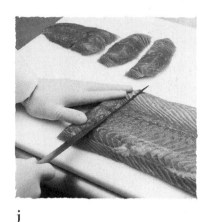

11. The finished fillet can be cut into portions of equal weight (j). This cut is known as a *tranche*.

j

The tail portion of the fillet tapers to become very thin. This piece can be made into a neat portion by using the technique shown here.

1. Score the flesh by slicing across the fillet just at the point where the fillet begins to thin. A chef's knife is pictured, but you could also use a filleting knife or a utility knife.

2. Fold the thinner end of the fillet under the thicker portion.

3. Gently shape the fillet with your hands to produce a piece that is the same approximate dimensions as the others cut from the whole fillet.

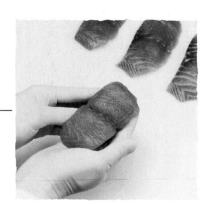

Lobster

Lobster is alive when you purchase it. The first step in preparing a lobster for boiling or steaming is to kill it. Lobsters can also be split before they are broiled or baked.

1. Leave the bands on the lobster's claws and lay it stomach down on a work surface. Insert the tip of a chef's knife into base of head (a).

2. Pull the knife all the way down through the shell, splitting the head in half (b).

3. Split the tail by reversing the direction of the lobster and positioning the tip of your chef's knife at the point where you made your initial cut. Cut through the shell of the tail section (c).

4. The lobster's tomalley and coral (if any) should be reserved and used as an ingredient in stuffings, sauces, or butters. Split lobsters can be stuffed and broiled, baked, or grilled (d).

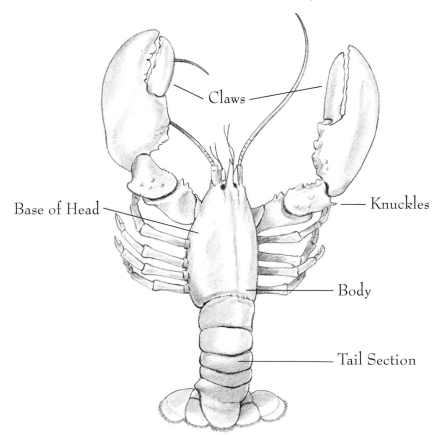

Claws

Knuckles

Base of Head

Body

Tail Section

a

b

c

d

Lobster—continued ▶

The edible meat can be removed from a cooked lobster as shown here to produce a large tail portion, intact claw sections, and smaller pieces from the knuckles and legs.

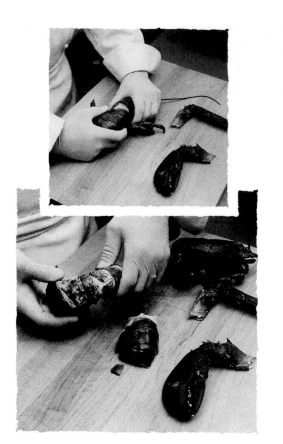

◀ Hold the tail section securely in one hand; hold the body of the lobster with the other. Twist your hands in opposite directions, pulling the tail away from the body. Pull out the tail meat out of the shell. It should come away in one piece.

Use the heel of the knife to crack the claws. Use your fingers to pry the shell away from the meat. The claw meat should also come out in a single piece, retaining the shape of the claw. ▶

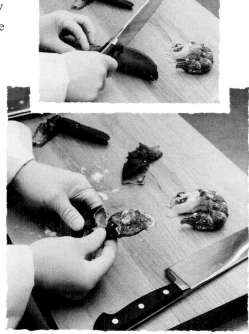

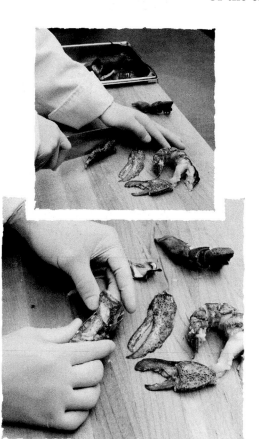

◀ Use your chef's knife to cut through the lobster knuckles. Pull out the knuckle meat.

To clean shrimp, you must remove the shells and the intestinal tract, or vein, a process known as deveining. Shrimp shells pull easily away from the shrimp meat. The shells can be reserved for other uses, such as making shrimp stock, bisque, and shellfish butters. The vein, which runs along the edge of the shrimp, is easy to locate.

After the shell is removed, lay the shrimp on a work surface, with the curved outer edge of the shrimp on the same side as your cutting hand. Slice into the shrimp with a paring or utility knife. The cut should be quite shallow for deveining, deeper if you are butterflying the shrimp. After you have made the cut, twist the knife blade to scrape out the intestinal tract. ▶

To remove the vien without cutting the shrimp, use a toothpick or skewer to "hook" the vein. Pull the vein out completely. The shrimp is now ready to poach for shrimp cocktail, or for other presentations. ▶

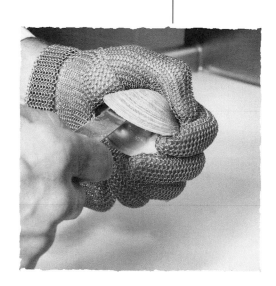

Clams and oysters are often served on the half shell, so it is important to be able to open them with ease. In addition, freshly shucked oysters and clams are often used for cooked dishes, such as oysters Rockefeller and clams casino.

Clams and oysters have a top and bottom shell held together by a hinge. The method for opening clams calls for the edge of a clam knife to be inserted between the shells. To open an oyster, the tip of an oyster knife is inserted directly into the hinge.

Scrub all mollusks well with a brush under cold running water before opening them. Any shellfish that remain open when tapped must be discarded because they are dead. If the shell feels unusually heavy or light, it should be checked. Occasionally, empty shells or shells filled with clay or sand are found.

Be sure to reserve any juices; these are sometimes referred to as *liquor* and they add great flavor to soups, stews, and stocks.

Opening Clams

1. Wear a wire mesh glove to hold the clam. Place the clam in your hand so that the hinged side is toward your palm. Work the side of a clam knife into the seam between the upper and lower shells. The fingers of your gloved hand can be used both to help guide the knife and to give extra force.

2. Twist the blade slightly as you would a key in a lock to pry open the shell.

3. When the clamshell opens, slide the knife over the inside of the top shell to release the clam from the shell. Make a similar stroke to release the clam from the bottom shell.

Opening Oysters

1. Wear a wire mesh glove to hold the oyster. Position the oyster so that the hinged side is facing outward. Work the tip of an oyster knife into the hinge, holding the upper and lower shells together, and twist it to break open the hinge.

2. Once the shell opens, slide the knife over the inside of the top shell to release the oyster from the shell. Make a similar stroke to release the oyster from the bottom shell.

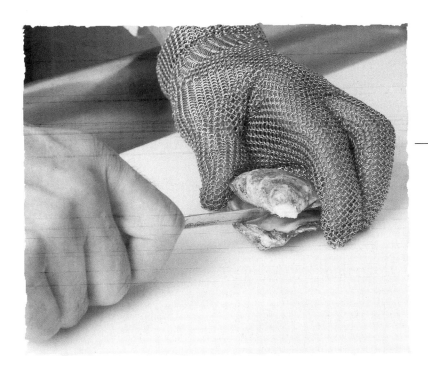

Summary

When you watch a professional magic act, you may find yourself awed by the trick. You are a willing believer in the illusion created by the magician. If, however, you are a magician, you are no longer in awe of the trick itself; you are astonished instead by the skill and finesse of the magician—the ease, the apparent effortlessness of motion.

Chefs are a great deal like magicians. To the novice, the transformation of a carrot to a pile of perfectly even julienne is almost miraculous. To the seasoned chef, the miracle is the skill, the coordination, and the rhythm of the right tool in an accomplished hand.

Glossary

Alloy: A homogeneous mixture of two or more metals.

Arkansas stone: A hard, smooth stone quarried from the Ozark Mountains in Arkansas. Used for sharpening knives.

Balance: The way that the weight in a knife is distributed between blade and handle. The balance point is where the blade meets the handle.

Blade: The portion of a knife that is used for cutting, slicing, and chopping.

Bolster: The thick band of steel between the body of the blade and the handle. Also referred to as the *shank*.

Boning knife: A knife of varying length and flexibility used primarily in the butchering and fabrication of meat, poultry, and sometimes fish.

Bronze: An alloy of copper and tin.

Bronze Age: The time in human history when bronze was the preferred metal for tools and knives, about 3500 B.C.E.

Carbon steel: An alloy of carbon and steel used to make knife blades; takes a good edge and resists discoloration and staining.

Carborundum stone: A sharpening stone available in various grits to sharpen knives to the desired degree of fineness. Man-made abrasive material used in the manufacture of sharpening stones.

Carving knife: A knife used to carve cooked meats.

Ceramic: A nonmetallic mineral compound (usually clay) formed and hardened by firing at high temperatures.

Chef's knife: An all-purpose knife used for chopping, slicing, and mincing. The blade is usually between 8 and 14 inches long. Also referred to as *French knife* and cook's knife.

Chinese cleaver: An all-purpose cleaver typically sharpened on one side of the blade.

Cleaver: A cutting tool with a large, rectangular blade; available in a range of sizes and weights. Butcher's cleavers are heavy enough to cut through bones and joints. Asian-style cleavers are used in the same applications as a chef's knife.

Cross-contamination: The spread of bacteria or other pathogens from one food or surface to another through improper handling and sanitary procedures.

Diamond-impregnated steel or stone: A sharpening or honing tool with industrial-grade diamonds over its surface.

Edge: The sharp part of the knife blade that runs from tip to tang and does the cutting.

Ergonomics: The study of how workspace and equipment design affects productivity.

Fillet knife: A flexible-bladed knife used for filleting fish.

Flat-ground: A knife edge formed by grinding an angle at the base of a uniformly thick blade, as opposed to tapering the blade.

Forge: To form metal blades through heating and hammering metal ingots into the correct shape.

French knife: See *chef's knife*.

Full tang: An extension of the blade into the handle that runs the full length and width of the handle.

Grinding: Producing an edge on a blade using a rotating abrasive surface, usually a belt or wheel.

Grit: Degree of coarseness of a sharpening stone or steel.

Guiding hand: The hand that holds the item being cut and acts as a guide to the knife blade.

Guard: The metal piece between the handle and the steel of a sharpening steel.

HACCP: Acronym for Hazard Analysis of Critical Control Points; a method of preventing foodborne disease by identifying potentially hazardous control points in the flow of food products through the production process and designing the process to eliminate contamination.

Handle: The part of the knife that is held; it is made of varying materials, including wood, wood impregnated with plastic, plastic, rubberlike compounds, and textured steel.

Heel: The back edge of the knife closest to the handle, used for tough jobs where weight and strength are required, such as cutting hard vegetables, bones, and shells.

High-carbon stainless steel: A metal that contains a high percentage of carbon up to 1.5 percent in relation to stainless steel. May also contain iron, chromium, molybdenum, and vanadium.

Hollow-ground: An edge formed by grinding into the blade at a concave angle, creating a very thin but sharp edge.

Hone: To sharpen on a fine-grained whetstone or on a steel.

Iron: A heavy metal used as the base in steel alloys; malleable when hot.

Mineral oil: A clear, mineral-based oil that may be used to lubricate sharpening stones.

Molybdenum: A hard, silvery-white metallic element used to strengthen and harden steel alloys.

Paring knife: A small knife with a blade ranging in length from 2 to 4 inches; used primarily for trimming and peeling vegetables.

Partial tang: An extension of a knife's blade that extends partway into the handle.

Rat-tail tang: A narrow extension of the knife blade (similar in shape to a rod) into the handle.

Rivets: The pieces used to attach the handle to the blade of a knife.

Rockwell scale: A scale used to measure the hardness of metals.

Shaft: The part of a steel used to steel knives.

Shank: See *bolster*.

Sharpening stone: A stone used to sharpen the edge of a dull knife.

Slicer: A long knife with a relatively thin blade, used principally for carving and slicing larger cuts of cooked, roasted, and smoked items.

Sintering: Fusing parts of a knife from different metals.

Spine: The top of the knife blade.

Stamp: To cut a shape from a sheet of metal.

Stainless steel: Carbon steel with chromium added to inhibit rust and discoloration.

Steel: 1. A tool used to maintain the knife's edge between sharpenings. It is sometimes referred to as a **sharpening** or **honing** steel. It is usually made of steel but may be ceramic, glass, or diamond-impregnated metal. 2. Metal; an alloy of iron, usually with the addition of carbon (carbon steel) and perhaps several other metals, including nickel, chromium, and molybdenum, to increase the hardness and/or resilience of the iron.

Steeling: Realigning, straightening, or maintaining the edge of a knife by passing the blade over the shank of a steel.

Stone: See *sharpening stone.*

Stone Age: The first known period of human culture, characterized by the use of stone tools.

Tang: The section of the knife blade that extends into the handle.

Taper-ground: A knife edge formed from a single sheet of metal that tapers smoothly from the spine of the knife to the cutting edge.

Tempering: The process of heating and cooling metals and metal alloys in order to bring out desired traits such as strength, flexibility, and stain resistance.

Utility knife: A smaller, lighter version of the chef's knife; its blade is usually between 5 and 7 inches long.

Whetstone: A hard, fine-grained stone for honing tools; a general term for sharpening stones.

Index